Amsterdam

D1132061

An Amsterdam Travel Guide Written By A Local.

The Best Travel Tips By a Local.

Table of Contents

About our guides - why they are unique

As we traveled, we got really tired of the typical boring travel guides. In most cases, wikipedia was more interesting, more complete and more dynamic. Even better, we found, was when friends, or friends of friends who were "locals", gave us tips about our travel destinations, as these were far more interesting. This guide tries to do the same as the "ask a local", but it is (maybe!) better organized and more complete. In all our guides, we hire a "local" writer, and then we edit the result to be sure that the guide is complete, unique, fun and interesting. Typically we won't add too many maps or photos (just a few), since all of that is already available online. Instead, we give you unique and original content that you otherwise would have had trouble finding.

Since we use different writers for each city, you will see (after you fall in love with our guides and download more than one), that they are not at all standardized. As each city is different, so each "local" is different, and therefore each guide is different! And we, personally, really like that. Thanks for being here and we really hope that you like it. Enjoy!

Chapter 1: The Basics of Amsterdam – advice, tips and considerations

So you're going to Amsterdam? Great news! It's a fantastic, and fantastically beautiful, city. I only ever heard one person say that it wasn't beautiful and he was strange (he thought the most enjoyable part of learning a new language was its grammar). For the rest, the consensus, as far as I know, is universal. Still, it is a bustling city, with its own rules, both written and unwritten, that you should probably be aware of when you go there. So make sure you at least read the basics.

Amsterdam – how to get there

Probably the easiest way to get to Amsterdam is to fly. Schiphol is an international airport and though it isn't Frankfurt, it isn't far off. That means there are almost always budget airlines in and out of town. If you plan a few weeks to a few months ahead, chances are good you can get there and back for a pittance. For example,

I justdid the most basic of searches, using skyscanner (a great site) and found a ticket there and back from London for less than a $50 US. A steal!

The Airport is situated 15km south-west of the city. To get to the city center from there is as easy as it is convenient. There is a direct train to Amsterdam Centraal Station, which will set you back €3.90, or €7.80 for a same-day return (though why you'd only want to go for one day is beyond me). The trip takes 20 minutes. From 5 AM to 1 AM the next day there are 6-7 trains per hour in both directions. Between the hours of 1 and 5 there is only one train per hour. Check online for the exact schedule.

Note that it's cheaper to get the ticket from the ticket machine; if you purchase your ticket at the counter you will pay €0.50 extra. There are plenty of ticket machines available. They accept credit and debit cards. Some also accept cash – these machines are bigger than the other machines and have a coin slot, so they're quite easy to spot.Alternatively, you can buy a Amsterdam Travel Ticket, which costs 15, 20, or 25 euros for one, two, or three days of travel and includes a train ticket to and from Schiphol to any of Amsterdam's stations, plus unlimited travel on all GVB trams, metros and (night)busses. All these train tickets are valid on almost all trains, except the Thalys.

Photo Credit 3: "Ticket Vending Machines" by Maartensteenhagen Licensed under Public Domain via Wikimedia Commons

If you are staying near Museumplein or Leidseplein, another choice is to use the Amsterdam Airport Express bus to the city center, which takes about 30 minutes. The fare is €5 for a single journey, €10 for a round trip ticket. You can also get an "Amsterdam ə Region Day Ticket", which costs €13.50. The Amsterdam Airport Express bus departs every 15 minutes from platform B9 (the bus platform, not the train platform) until midnight. Thereafter there is one bus per hour.

Not fussed about money? Then a taxi will get you wherever you need to go. The ride costs about €50. Depending on the time of day and traffic levels, it can take anywhere from 25 to 50 minutes. Yes that's longer than a train, but then you'll be dropped off at the doorstep of your hotel, with the train you'll still have to go from Centraal Station to wherever you're staying. Another option is the Connexxion Hotel Shuttle. This shuttle connects over 100 city center hotels. It departs every 30 minutes from 6am to 9pm. A single ticket is €15. They are more convenient than the train, especially if you're one of those people who drags around seven suitcasesbecause you really needed that seventh pair of shoes for your weekend trip, but it is still cheaper than a taxi.

Driving to Amsterdam is also a good choice, though make sure you aren't driving near one of the big cities, like Utrecht, Amsterdam or Eindhoven, at rush hour, as traffic slows to a crawl. Outside of these hours, the Netherlands has great road network, with clear signage, so getting around is easy and convenient. Be aware that if you are traveling to Amsterdam by car, it might be wise to park somewhere outside the city. Traffic in Amsterdam is dense, parking spaces are really expensive and nearly impossible to find, and the roads are a hell of one-way streets and mysterious, unexpected turnings.

Instead follow the P+R, or Park and Ride, signs, to parking lots equipped with trams and buses straight into town. On the A10 motorway you can follow the signs east to Zeeburg P+R, or head south-east to get to the ArenAP+R, south to the OlympischStadionP+R, and to the west there is SloterdijkP+R.

If you're really desperate to park your car in town, you can use the different parking websites to find out about prices and available parking garages in the city itself. On Prettigparkeren (comfortable parking) you can find a nice overview of all the public parking garages in the city and the prices they charge. A final option is to drive into Amsterdam Noord, above the IJ river (pronounced 'aye'), where parking is free, and then then take a quick ferry ride (also free) to the city center. One good spot to park is Ijplein (something like 'aye plain'), which you can reach from the Amsterdam ring road.

Finally, there are trains and in truth these aren't a bad choice either. Trains in Amsterdam are frequent and on time. The biggest advantage here is probably that they drop you off right in the middle of town, at Centraal station. There are some night trains to other cities in the Netherlands, but I would recommend you study their routs carefully, because they sometimes can take hours to take you a distance that would normally take you 20 minutes (they tend to do loops).

Do I need to speak Dutch?

No, you don't. In fact, the Dutch pride themselves on their ability with languages. On average they speak 3.2, and will automatically switch over to something they think you'll understand – usually English, when they notice you're foreign. This can be frustrating for those people who actually want to learn the language, as the moment somebody has a slight accent or stumbles even a little bit in their pronunciation of Dutch, they Dutch will switch.

In fact, I had a friend who was an English professor (as in, actually from England, not a professor in English) and, even after living in the country for ten years, he did not speak Dutch. When we asked him about it, rather accusingly I might add, he exploded in rage – something that's rare for the English – and said, 'None of you will practice Dutch with me!' We looked at each other, shrugged and continued in English. It was true, of course, but none of us were going to listen to him mangle our languages just so he could get some practice.

Bicycle paths are for bikes and bicycles don't make any noise

A lot of tourists, when they first arrive in Amsterdam, see the city's sidewalks and think, 'wow, the sidewalks in this country are so wide! And look at these wonderful smooth brown surfaces that I can roll my wheelie bag down. They must really like tourists here.' They proceed to merrily wander down these paths, pulling their heavy, 10 cubic meter suitcases behind them. Their fun is soon spoiled however, when the Dutch on their bicycles swerve past at neck-breaking speed and starts screaming obscenities. 'Get on the damned road!' the tourists think to themselves, 'Don't you have any respect for pedestrians?' Even while the Dutch people on their bikes are screaming at them, in Dutch, to get the hell off the bike paths.

Don't be one of those people. Yes, your wheelie bag won't roll down the normal sidewalk quite as well, due to those annoying cobbles which look so picturesque at a distance, but are actually hell to pull bags across (to not even mention what they do ankles in high heels). Yet angry people on bikes nearly smashing into you and then suggesting you have carnal relations with a member of your family is a lot worse.

Also, remember that bicycles don't make any noise! This means that when you cross the road you, just like your mommy told you, have to look both ways! It is a heart stopping experience to have somebody nearly run into you with a bicycle. To have them actually run into you can be a vacation stopping experience. You have been warned.

By Hide-sp (Hide-sp's file) CC BY-SA 2.5 via Wikimedia
Commons

The weather – or what to talk about in Amsterdam when you have nothing else to talk about

Amsterdam and her people are at their best when the weather is nice. Unfortunately, you never know when that's going to be. What most people don't realize is that Amsterdam is at about the same latitude as Siberia. This – despite the Gulf Stream delivering heat from the Caribbean – means that it can be rainy and windy into the heart of summer. Heck, sometimes summer even skips a year, just to keep you guessing! This doesn't just affect the décor, but the mood to, with the people turning miserable, surly and snappish. That isn't really that strange. After all, how would you feel if you haven't seen the sun for so long that you've forgotten what shape it is?

Yes, that is as miserable as it sounds. There is nothing quite as bad, or as horrible, as driving home in the whipping rain, on you bicycle in the middle of July. This goes double on those days where the gusting wind has taught the rain to fly sideways. At the same time, those days are well compensated for when the first days of spring finally do arrive. Something truly magical happens on those first days where the sun is out. People flock to the terraces, which cling to the side of every street and crowd the side of every canal, and will camp out on them as long as there's even a single ray of sunlight, even if they need to wear winter coats and gloves to do so!

Then, on one of the first days that the sun is accompanied with the first glimmers of warmth, all the women of the city collectively decide (I suspect they've got an app for it) the winter wardrobe is done and it is time for spring clothing. In Dutch this is called 'Rokjes dag', or 'short skirt day' and it is better than the weather man at announcing spring's arrival.

From there it's a kind of festival. Offices empty, barbecues come out and for as long as the sun is out people will take to blankets and occupy every patch of grass the city parks – or 'Amsterdam's back gardens' as they're colloquially known – have to offer. In the middle of summer, this can be a long time indeed. You see, there is one advantage of being so far north and that is that when summer does roll around, the sun comes up at five in the morning and doesn't set till eleven at night. For those who like a party, many are the opportunities in the middle of summer – when the city is buzzing, the mood giddy and the parties numerous – that you can find yourself stumbling home, shielding your eyes from the sun's glare and cursing yourself for a fool for again not having brought your sunglasses.

Winter, on the other hand, isn't quite as glorious an affair. If you're thinking, 'Wouldn't Amsterdam, with all its pretty canals and buildings, be beautiful covered under a blanket of snow?' You'd be absolutely right. The only problem is, you don't know when that's going to be either. That Gulf Stream mentioned earlier means that the temperature frequently doesn't drop below freezing. Don't misunderstand, it can. You just don't know when, or if, it will. When it does, and the canals freeze over, it is exactly as beautiful as you imagined – possibly more so. People grab their skates (a favorite past time in the Netherlands) and take to the canals in their thousands. Inventive entrepreneurs start selling Dutch snacks, like pea soup, hot chocolate and sweet tea, on the ice itself and for a few days you can see the talented swirl ballerina-like between the amateurs, who spend more time on their ass than on their skates.

Unfortunately, you just can't predict when this is going to happen. The canals most certainly don't freeze over every year. And if you get it wrong, well then you'll have to wander through the wind and the driving rain along with the locals. People say that you should explore Amsterdam on a bike, if you have the chance.

by Amsterdam Municipal Department for the Preservation and Restoration of Historic Buildings and Sites (bMA)CC BY-SA 2.5 via Wikimedia Commons)

Well, when the weather is like this, don't. There is nothing quite as miserable or as cold as riding a bicycle through a wind storm that seems to be convinced you need to be going the other way. The Dutch often say that the wind never seems to blow your way. On a bicycle this is actually true. It's always in your face and carrying water droplets with it with enough force that they sting. What's more, though the temperature might be just above freezing, the wind factor and the rain make it so that it feels like it is well below.

If you do manage to get caught in one of these on a bicycle, you've got the undesirable choice of covering your face and not seeing where you're going, or seeing where you're going and not being able to feel your face when you get there. Umbrellas aren't up to the challenge either. The wind gusts, snaps and pulls, like a psychopathic child, bent on destroying everything you love in this world (and trust me, you'll love your umbrella when the weather is like this). For a while you think you've got the hang of it, turning the umbrella into the wind to keep it whole, but then the wind will turn tricky, reverse, and suddenly your umbrella gets turned inside out and all you're holding a funnel. Then you're left with unenviable task of trying to push the damned thing back into a more useful shape, all without bending those flimsy metal things that make up the umbrella's skeleton, even while the weather gleefully uses these moments to pour copious amounts of water down the back of your coat.

So what I'm saying is, on days like this take public transportation, a taxi, or maybe just avoid the country entirely. You can see what the weather predictions are going to be like online. They're actually pretty decent most of the time. There's this site called 'buienradar.nl' or 'rain radar' that all the locals use. It dares to make up to the minute predictions about when the next rain storm will hit. And generally they're right! Now if that isn't Dutch efficiency at its best, then I don't know what is. Of course, it would be even better if instead of predicting the weather they'd learn to control it. But we're not there yet.

The Dutch police are civil servants – emphasis of civil

Unlike in many other countries, the Dutch police force is generally both civil and polite. They are a great source of information and are by and large very helpful. If you have a question, don't hesitate to ask them. They don't mind and they generally will know the answer too! Of course, there are limits. If they're wrestling somebody to the ground, they might not be willing to stop and tell you were the Ann Frank house is.

Barring that it's you they're wrestling to the ground, they can often be negotiated with! If you get caught doing something you shouldn't, you can frequently get off with only a warning if you deal with them respectfully. For those not familiar with this practice, that means – among other things – not shouting at them, comparing them to genitals or animals, or trying to steal their guns. Any of these activities will not go down well. The thing to remember is that just because in some places the police are megalomaniacs with control issues,this isn't necessarily true everywhere. Try speaking to them nicely first. It's always possible to switch to shouting and vulgarities later. Switching the other way, I've found, is generally far less effective.

By nl:User:Gvdbor (Own work by nl:User:Gvdbor) [Public domain], via Wikimedia Commons

Short cuts and how not to get lost (which is harder than you may think)

In the olden days, before there were map apps (which have spoiled our fun a little bit), it was actually very hard not to get lost unless you either knew the city well, or were very good at reading a map and had a fantastic sense of direction. You see, Amsterdam doesn't believe in straight. After all, who needs easy navigation? Instead, the city was designed to look like half a spider's web, with five long canals curving from the Brouwersgrachtin the north-west, down and around, like a set of boomerangs, towards the Amstel in the south-east. These canals are then intersected by other canals that shoot out, like the spokes of a wheel.

The curve of these main canals, and the strange angles, twists and turns of the roads in the center that result, mean that unless you're paying very close attention, you can end up facing one way, when you are absolutely convinced you're facing another. Obviously, this completely screws with your sense of direction. So much so, that even a momentary lapse of concentration will have you heading in completely the opposite direction of where you wanted to go. And these lapses of attention are actually quite easy, as there is a lot to see and get distracted by. What's more, even though the city is incredibly beautiful, there is no denying that the streets are all a bit similar, after all, almost every building is old, beautiful, tall and fitted with narrow windows without curtains. This means that navigating by landmarks can be tough as well.

Fun fact! Due to the curves of the streets it is often possible to get to somewhere on the street you are on faster by taking several side streets than by just following the main street! Occasionally this can save you hours of walking. You just have to know which shortcut to take. The only problem is that often tourists don't know those shortcuts. I've met visitors to the city who had spent days walking an hour to get from their hotel to their favorite destination and an hour back, even though the total round trip didn't need to take more than fifteen minutes if they'd just taken the right shortcut. This is great fun to point out as a local – less enjoyable if you're the tourist on the other side of the conversation.

So, to cut a long story short (horrible pun), make sure you have a good map – or even better, google maps or something similar loaded into your phone! It might be cheating, but this is a vacation, damn it! Cheating is allowed! (Just to be clear, I meant on maps, not your partners).

Coffeeshops, magic mushrooms and why marijuana isn't legal

The Dutch don't actually smoke a lot of weed. Yes, you might have heard that they do, or at least thought it, based on the number of coffeeshops, or marijuana cafes, you see when you're wandering about the city, but it just isn't that popular – nor are there that many coffee shops, really. There are only 183 coffeeshops currently operating in Amsterdam, a number that's expected be brought down to 155 soon. In comparison, there are more than a thousand cafes. What's more, a great number of these coffeeshops cater to tourists only, with some estimates suggesting that 90% of the people in coffeeshops are, in fact, not Dutch. Mind you, it could be that the Dutch are just more likely to consume in the comfort of their own homes, while tourists hang out and smoke in the coffee shops, so don't take that number too seriously.

Dutch drug policies are centered on the idea that people should make their own decisions about how they treat their own bodies, as long as in so doing they don't harm anybody else. Another guiding principal is that persecuting drug users doesn't prevent drug use, but only serves to push it underground. And once drug use is underground and stigmatized, they become far harder to control and influence and when things go wrong, users will not turn to the police for either justice or medical assistance. For that reason, the Dutch government handles what is called a 'gedoogbeleid' which is a really long word that means, it's not legal, but we'll tolerate it as long as you behave responsibly.

Do note that production, trading and stocking drugs remain a criminal offense, as in any other country, except if you have a coffeeshop license. Yes, that is as weird as it sounds, as it means coffeeshops can sell weed, but can't buy it. Nor can they have more than a small amount on the premises. Of course, everybody knows that this doesn't actually work and the authorities accept that the coffeeshops are constantly bringing in product from their warehouses and wholesalers, both of which are illegal. And yes, this does mean that in some ways Dutch drug laws are now no longer in the vanguard of world drug policies, with some countries, like Portugal and even the USA, havingmore liberal drug policies. Let's just say the conservatives have been in power for a while.

That aside, the basic idea of how drugs should be treated is sound. The Dutch have accepted that marijuana – and other drugs for that matter – should be treated like the use of tobacco and alcohol, and in fact not very dissimilar to problems of obesity, gambling addiction and such. They also point to the fact that prohibition of alcohol in the US in the years 1919-1933 didn't work at all either and ultimately had to be retracted.

All this means that the police will let you buy in coffeeshops, though the sales are limited to five grams per transaction and they won't sell to minors.What it does not mean, however, is that you can just sit on a terrace, or a bar for that matter, and spark up a joint. Many bar and restaurant managers in Amsterdam don't like you doing this one bit and will ask you to leave. When they do so, they are in their right. Those bars and terraces are not designated places. Officially, neither are the parks, or the streets, but nobody really seems to mind it much if you smoke there. Still, if for some reason police officers takes issue with you smoking out in the open and asks you put out the joint, you should do as they say. Screaming 'it's my right' is both unhelpful and, more importantly, wrong.

As mentioned, the Dutch don't smoke much. As a whole, have one of the lowest marijuana consumption rates in the world, with only 16% of people having smoked weed by the age of 28. Statistically speaking the Dutch smoke only half the weed than Americans do per capita. In fact, many Dutch people kind of look down on the practice. For the Dutch, it's something that some people do as a teenager, but then you're expected to grow out of it. Whether
this is because of the fact that it's been semi-legal for several decades now, or because of some other reason, is as yet unclear.

Maybe the experiments going on in Portugal and several states in American well shed more light on the matter.

Then there are magic mushrooms, or padoes, which comes from the Dutch word for mushrooms, paddestoelen. For the longest time these weren't even considered drugs and were sold is so called 'smart shops' along with popular natural medicines as Ginkgo Biloba, Guarana, food additives and vitamins. Then, after a number of widely publicized cases where magic mushrooms were reputedly responsible for a number of deaths and emergencies (something that was never actually the case, but the media loves a good drug story), the government initiated research after research into the effect of the mushrooms, each returning back the result that they were not dangerous.

Finally, one said that there was a slight risk, as you could never be sure of a mushroom's strength and at high doses they could cause trouble for liver and kidneys. The conservative government used this as an excuse to ban them. The group who'd done the study used actually stated that they found it unfortunate that the government had decided to use their study the way they had and that they did not back the government's decision.

Fortunately, the ban did not include the truffle, which – though slightly weaker – has the advantage that its strength is far less variable from one truffle to the next. This means you might need more, but at least you know exactly what you're getting. These are still on sale and – as I've been told by one man who grows them – they are getting stronger, as they same expertise that was put into mushrooms is now being directed at them.

Note that hard drugs, though readily available, are illegal. At the same time, the government has accepted that it is better to treat addiction as an illness than a moral wrong and as a result has been operating treatment programs and needle exchanges since the mid-eighties. Another program they've long operated is the testing of ecstasy pills without the risk of prosecution, so that users know what theyare putting into their bodies, as quite frequently people put all kinds of crap into those things.

If you are looking for hard drugs, do not buy from street dealers, particularly the ones in the Red Light District. There was an incident several years ago where heroin was sold as cocaine and several tourists died from overdoses. Signs went up all over the city, with the police warning about this incident and offering numbers to call in case you thought something similar had happened to you. They also stated that they would not prosecute you if you did get in touch, which was another great example of Dutch enlightened drug policies – where the held belief is that it's better to save a life, than catch a criminal.

Windmills – The Netherlands wouldn't have gotten anywhere without them

The windmills have such a big importance in the Netherlands that they have their own national holiday, on May 11th. Throughout Dutch history, the enemies of Don Quixote have been used in many ways. The one they're best known for is to free up more land.

26% of modern-day Netherlands is actually under the sea level! That's like standing up to you knees in sea water. Okay, it's nothing like that, but it's a nice image. I'm imagining yellow rain boots.

The way the Dutch keep that land free of water is mainly through dikes, but of course that's not enough. If you build a dike, then all you've done is divide one area of water into two. After you've built the dike, you still need to get rid of the water. The Dutch devised a way to use wind, as this was considered more effective than a bunch of guys running up and down throwing water from one side to the other. Of course, because dikes are permeable, water keeps seeping through and so the windmills had to keep turning. That's why the Netherlands for such a long time had so many more windmills than any other country.

Later they also served as an important part of the first industrial revolution, when the Netherlands used them to saw wooden planks for their boats (something that before that time was done with muscle power alone). This meant that the Dutch could saw wood twenty times(!) faster than places where men did the work. This allowed the Dutch the build enough ships to rival the fleets of much bigger countries, like England and France. Interestingly it took them nearly a hundred years to go from using windmills to suck up water to using them to saw wood. The problem was that nobody could quite figure out how to transform a round motion into a back and forth one. Only when somebody solved that problem, could windmills turn the Netherlands into a world power.

Contrary to popular belief, you don't even have to leave Amsterdam to see a windmill up close. Like most things, Amsterdam has a few of them on your doorstep or just a short bike ride away. There are in fact eight windmills at the heart of Amsterdam. For 17th century molens (Dutch for windmill), head for De 1200 Roe, De 1100 Roe or the Riekermolen. For later examples of molen artistry, try D'Admiraal or De Bloem, which has been moved from its original location.Then there are the Molen van Sloten and de Otter.

If you are into architectural makeovers, like beer, or are just a bit lazy, visit de Gooyer or Fuenmolen. This windmill, in the east of Amsterdam, actually houses a beer brewery! Bierbrouwerij't, as it's called, still sells the traditional Dutch Ijmeer (aye lake) beer, among many others. Quite a few of the beers are quite tasty. Probably the best way to go is to first order their tasters, which lets you sample all their beers, and then see where you go from there (probably you'll end up slipping off your bench if you're doing it alone as they're quite strong). As a special treat, if you're around on the first Saturday of the month, head on down, as the mill will actually be working!

Finding what you're looking for – where stay, eat or drink

In truth, though the city is old, where eat, drink and stay are, like most thriving metropolises, constantly changing and whatever I wrote here would be outdated by the time you've read it. Instead, therefore, let me tell you where to look, so that you can get the information you need.

Tripadvisor is, like always, an incredibly useful tool to know what people have to say about where to eat, stay or drink, as the places are rated by the people visiting them, rather than the places themselves. The Dutch have a similar service, called Iens.nl. Obviously, it's in Dutch, but you should be able to figure it out (Google translate can help). The scores are pretty straight forward, as long as you know they're out of ten. And they'll be by locals rather than tourists!

One thing I always tend to do when using tools like these is look at the ages of the people giving the positive and the negative ratings – I've found that younger people are generally more exuberant about where they've been, possibly because they don't have as much experience. I've also found that older audiences are far more critical and far more likely to complain about things that other people would take in stride. For that reason, when reading reviews, I tend to take younger people's opinions with a grain of salt when they're exceedingly positive, while I take older people's reviews less seriously when they're overly negative.

Another great tool for finding places to stay Booking.com. I've used this site myself numerous times and have found great deals, where expensive hotels have gone for half price, during off season. This is a very good tool to check out. I advise using it either far ahead of when you're planning to go, or only a few days (or even only 24 hours) ahead. This way you'll either get them trying to fill up their rooms in advance, or trying to fill up their rooms at the last minute. In both cases you're going to get good deals. I once stayed in a five star hotel for $60. They even upgraded me! The room I ended up in was so big, they could have played a football game inside! (I'm Dutch, I compare everything to football).

Alternatively, for places to stay make sure you check out AirBnB, as I know a lot of Dutch people who are looking to make an extra buck, who have put their apartments, houses and even houseboats on this site. In some ways, using AirBnB will give you a far more homely experience, as you'll generally have a kitchen, a bed and a place to relax. It will often also give you a lot more privacy, as nobody will be snooping around your room pretending to clean it, or checking who you're bringing up, like they do at many hotels.

Finally, IAMsterdam.com is a great site, where the city has done a fantastic job of outlining all the possibilities and opportunities the city has to offer, in terms of parties, food, museums and sites. The site is available in English. So make sure you spend a bit of time nosing through there as well!

Chapter 2: The city's history – from marsh to metropolis

It isn't exactly clear how far back you have to go to say 'this is when Amsterdam started'. There is evidence from recent excavations accompanying the building of the fifth metro line that suggest the area was inhabited as far back as 2600 BC. They found pole-axes, stone hammers and some pottery, which all dating from the Neolithic era (New Stone Age). But you can't really say that that was when the city started. That's a bit like saying the US was founded when the Native Americans moved in. For one thing, pottery does not a city make, for another there is no evidence that the area that would become the city was constantly inhabited from this time.

The founding of a city

A date that is on a much firmer footing, if you'll excuse the pun, is the 12th century AD. At that time fishermen living along the marshy banks of the Amstel River built a bridge across the Amstel, near the IJ – which at the time was a saltwater inlet. Soon afterwards they built a wooden lock below it, to protect their homes from flooding by the rising IJ-waters. They, in other words, dammed the Amstel. And so a city name was born. Of course, it wasn't called 'Amsterdam' right from the get go. A document from the October 27th, 1275 AD reports the settlement's name as 'Aemstelredamme'. Apparently the people in this area have always liked long names. The document, interestingly enough, was by Count Floris V and exempted the people from paying a bridge toll. Okay, maybe that's not that interesting. I wonder if it was for their own bridge.

It took another fifty years or so for the name to change to its modern-day version. City rights, however, were earned much sooner, in 1306 AD, when they were given by Gwijde van Henegouwen, bishop of Utrecht. What are city rights, you ask? Good question! They're nothing like what they are today, that's for sure. For one thing, they have nothing to do with population size (there's one city in the Netherlands, called Staverden, that has 40 people). Basically, in the middle ages rulers were constantly looking to raise funds in the short term, to fund wars, parties or marriages. Communities that wanted to get out from under the ruler's thumb would offer to give the rulers a lot of money to receive special rights.

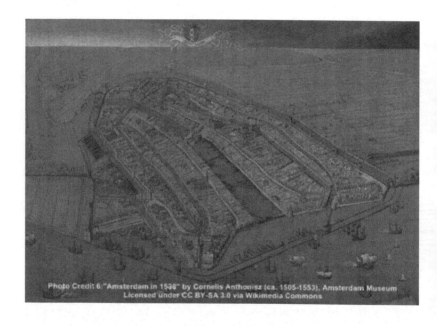

Photo Credit 6 "Amsterdam in 1538" by Cornelis Anthonisz (ca. 1505-1553), Amsterdam Museum Licensed under CC BY-SA 3.0 via Wikimedia Commons

These rights could include the privilege to hold markets, build walls, charge tolls and mint money. Also, the city could self-govern and the people in the city, unlike their rural cousins, were free to move around as much as they liked. Hence the expression 'stadsluchtmaaktvrij', or 'city air makes free'. It might have made you free, but it also frequently made you sick, as most cities thought it was perfectly reasonable to combine streets with sewers. The first closed off sewer system (if you ignore the Romans) wasn't built till the late 19th century, in London and even while it was built huge numbers of people maintained that it was a huge waste of money. Go figure, aye?

Back to Amsterdam: In the 14th century on Amsterdam truly began to flourish, mainly through trade with the Hanseatic League. The product that started it all was beer. Could that be why the Dutch still drink so much of it? Then, in 1345, an alleged Eucharistic miracle in the Kalverstraat(some guy claimed he saw something in the flames as he lay dying) rendered the city an important place of pilgrimage, with many of the pilgrims that made the journey ultimately settling down in the city. Of course, the protestant reformation put an end to all that, but by that time the city was large enough that it could attract new blood on its own and didn't need the constant stream of pilgrims.

(Throughout most of human history cities were such a cesspit of violence, disease and famine that they needed a constant stream of immigrants from the countryside just to keep the city population steady).

Independence and the golden age

In the 16th century, the Dutch rebelled against Philip II of Spain and his successors. The main reasons for the uprising were the imposition of new taxes, the tenth penny, and the religious persecution of Protestants by the Inquisition. Although Amsterdam began the war on the Spanish side, possibly because they didn't want to lose their status as a place of pilgrimage, they ultimately changed sides with the Alteratie of 1578 and gave its support to William I of Orange. So why did they switch? Quite simply it was all about trade. On the catholic side Amsterdam's position as dominant trading city was slipping. Trade was (and still is) very important to Amsterdam.

Even after independence was won and Protestantism became the predominant religion, people remained free to believe what they wanted (within certain limits). For example, there is still a Roman Catholic minority around today. This religious tolerance served the city well, as around this time there were a great number of religious wars all across Europe and minorities were frequently persecuted. Amsterdam became a natural safe haven for people of all colors and stripes.

Rembrandt [Public domain], via Wikimedia Commons

This included Jews from the Iberian Peninsula, Huguenots from France, prosperous merchants and printers from Flanders and economic and religious refugees from the Spanish-controlled parts of the Low Countries. The influx of Flemish printers and the city's intellectual tolerance made Amsterdam a center for the European free press and innovation. This led to what is known as the Dutch golden age in 17th century. During this period Amsterdam became the wealthiest city in the world.

As already mentioned, innovations in windmill design, where the wind – rather than men – sawed the planks necessary to build ships, made it possible for Dutch ship builders to hugely speed up ship building.

The resulting fleet made it possible for the Dutch to project their influence from Amsterdam to the Baltic Sea, North America, and Africa, as well as present-day Indonesia, India, Sri Lanka, and Brazil. They formed the basis of a worldwide trading network with the city at its heart. Interestingly, where many other countries, like Spain and France, owned their fleets and their colonies directly, the Dutch created semi-private companies to do the work for them. These were known as Dutch East India Company and the Dutch West India Company. These two companies, which were run for profit, were far more effective than their government-controlled rivals, where the state was constantly interfering. For example, when Japan closed its borders it was only the Dutch that were still allowed to trade with them, as they didn't feel the need to try to impose their religious beliefs on everybody. This made the Netherlands capable of punching well above its weight. These companies acquired overseas possessions in Indonesia, South Africa and all over America, that later became Dutch colonies, some of which the crown still holds today. It was, in fact, the Dutch that founded New York, which was originally called 'New Amsterdam'. This all led to Amsterdam becoming Europe's most important port for the shipment of goods and the leading Financial Centre of the world.

Another innovation, in 1602, led to the creation of the first stock market, when the office of the Dutch East

India Company sold its own shares. You can still see the first stock exchange today. This, along with joined ventures in shipping, used to divide the cost of losing a ship at sea over a number of parties, so that it wasn't quite as crippling, in effect led to the creation of modern day capitalism. Yup, that was the Dutch. America had nothing to do with it. Hell, the USA didn't even exist at this point.So you can blame us for all of it. We were the 1%! Bet you didn't know that!

The Second World War – something embarrassing and something shameful

When the Second World War broke out, Amsterdam was completely unprepared. Years of pacifism and underfunding for the armed forces meant that the army, navy and air force were outdated, poorly equipped and undertrained. In a glorious example of only seeing what you want to see, the Dutch had received numerous warnings of impending doom, including the massive military build ups occurring in neighboring counties andinformation supplied by a German general about Germany's plans to attack, but these were not taken seriously. As a result, the Dutch were woefully underprepared.

Add to that that nobody had told them about this new invention called paratroopers, which could be dropped behind enemy lines, thereby rendering defensive structures all but impotent and you can imagine what kind of a fiasco the defense of the Netherlands turned into. The Germans predicted they'd be able to take the Netherlands in two days. The Dutch soldiers, through bravery alone, held out for five. Then, after the bombing of Rotterdam, the Netherlands surrendered; quite a long way to fall from one of the most powerful nations on earth, no?

(Public domain, via Wikimedia Commons

The loss of the war was embarrassing. What happened during the occupation was shameful. The Dutch, always fond of tallying and keeping track of everything, had kept detailed books on everybody's race, religion and parentage. Though the stories of the atrocities committed against the Jews in Germany had certainly reached the Dutch by this time, nobody took it upon themselves to burn these documents. As a result when the Nazis invaded, they just needed to find those listed as 'Jewish' and throw them onto the trains bound for the concentration camps. The Jewish community across the Netherlands was utterly decimated. More than 100,000 Jews were deported, famously including Anne Frank. Those Dutch citizens that harbored the Jews risked deportation themselves if they were caught. Many Dutch people did nothing. Even worse, quite a few ratted out their neighbors for rewards, special treatment, or just to get access to what the Jewish communities had.

By Unknown. [Public domain], via Wikimedia Commons

This is a shameful moment of Dutch history, to be sure. Fortunately, we have learned something from it, (though at far too high a price), with it now being illegal in the Netherlands for any official document to ask a person what religion they practice. Many other countries in the world have not followed the Dutch lead in this matter, however, with them still keeping track of what religion their citizens follow. This is unfortunate.

Though this might be a little bit of a serious tone to take for this guide, I would just like to say one thing. The Dutch experience should serve as a reminder that when a government tries to collect information or enact laws, the question that its people should ask is not, 'what will this government do with these laws or this information?' but rather, 'What could the worst government we can imagine do with these laws or this information?' And if they can imagine bad things happening, they should take to the streets. To do anything else is complacent at best and criminal at worst.

At the very end of the Second World War, when Germany was losing but only half of the Netherlands had been liberated, due to the failed military operation Market Gardens, we experienced what is known as the hunger winter. This winter was hard indeed, as a number of factors – including an exceptionally cold winter and the Nazi army purposefully destroying bridges and food transports as a reprisal for a train strike announced by the Dutch government in exile – combined to take a deadly toll. By its end the Dutch were down to about 400 grams of meat and a kilo of potatoes a week. There was no fuel to burn. Trees and antique furniture were used for heat, while dogs, cats, rats and tulip bulbs were eaten by the desperate population. By some estimates 20,000 people died.

After the war – Liberalism and protest

Because of the war and other incidents of the 20th century, almost the entire city centerof Amsterdam had fallen into disrepair. As society was changing, politicians and other influential figures took this opportunity to redesign large parts of it. There was an increasing demand for office buildings and new roads as the automobile became available to most common people. Many canals were filled in. Fortunately some of this road building has been turned back.

The 1960s and 1970s made Amsterdam themagisch centrum (magical center) of Europe, much like Berlin is (was?) today. The use of soft drugs was tolerated and this policy made the city a popular destination for hippies and alternative figures. Squatting became widespread and was even encourage with such policies as 'a bed, a chair and a table', where houses could be legally occupied if you managed to put these three things inside. Anarchists, such as the Provos and a local political movement Kabouterbeweging, wanted to change society. The squatting of empty buildings led to a strong confrontation with contractors, who became aligned with the Dutch Mafia and were willing, since the law didn't support them, to use violence to evict these undesirables. As you can guess, this led to violence.

A hippy bus (photo by Johannes AubeleLicenced under CC BY-SA 3.0 via Wikimedia Commons)

The city veered leftwards, even as the government, which represented more conservative elements, tried to maintain control. Riots and clashes with the police were frequent. From flower-power the town descended into something much darker. Distrust of authority became rife. This all came to a head when the city of Amsterdam knocked down huge swaths of housing and historical buildings to dig metro tunnels and build freeways, in the name of progress. This didn't go down very well with the population. More and more riots broke out.

Photo Credit 8: "Queen Beatrix during swearing" by Koen Suyk held by Nationaal Archief Via Wikimedia Commons

Amsterdam started the 1980s in an explosive manner, when, at the coronation of Queen Beatrix, protests outside the church turned ugly and fights broke out.

Things got so out of hand that the army ultimately had to be called in. The government partially retreated after this and halted the construction of the highway. Only the metros were finished. Meanwhile, large private organizations, such as Stadsherstel Amsterdam, were founded with the aim of restoring the city center.These initiatives were a great success, with the Grachtengordel joining the UNESCO World Heritage List in 2010. Those protesters of the 1980s must be proud of what they accomplished.

Liberalism slips away, while the Dutch look the other way

As noted, the height of Dutch liberalism occurred in the sixties, when the idea of 'live and let live' became the Dutch mindset. The idea being that if everybody was left to uphold their own philosophies, ideas and values, as long as they didn't interfere with anybody else's, people would be happy. And so immigrants were allowed to live as they liked, in their own enclaves and suburbs, without integrating into Dutch society. This philosophy came undone in 2001 when the Dutch first witnessed the attack on the World Trade Center in New York and soon after had one of their own film makers stabbed brutally to death in the street for exploring anti-Islamic sentiments in his movies.

Suddenly the Dutch realized that their idyllic philosophy of live and let live only works when all sides agreed to it and they came to believe that the Muslims did not, in fact, agree. With the fall of 'live and let live' the country took a sharp lurch to the right and became far less open to immigrants, especially from Islamic countries. Many people say that the Netherlands became a darker place that day. Now, to immigrate to the Netherlands is exceedingly hard – in fact, the conditions are among the hardest in Europe, with people that want the Dutch passport needing to reside in the country for seven years and pass tests to show they are 'Dutch' enough.

Chapter 3: The Dutch Culture, or why the Dutch have no curtains, are so brutally honest and yet never seem to get into fights

A lot of people think the Dutch are just Germans in (rather tall) disguises. The Dutch think nothing could be further from the truth. Though we no doubt have a lot in common with the Germans (including a language that makes us sound like we're constantly shouting at each other), the differences are just as numerous. For example, the Germans are far more hierarchical than the Dutch. Where titles and status are very important among our eastern neighbors, the Dutch are far more egalitarian. Legend has it that this is because when the waters came, everybody had to help fix the dikes, whether rich or poor, as otherwise everybody's houses would flood. I suspect this is just that, a legend, but that we are more egalitarian is certainly true. This shows itself in many different ways, such as the right of any Dutch person to disagree with any other, be they boss, parent, or university professor.

In fact, for any person not to let another person have their say is considered undutch indeed and will earn them the scorn of lookers on. This is why the Dutch will shout at each other in turn after an accident and why you're allowed to disagree with the police, who will generally let you have your say if you do so respectfully. This is also why the Dutch don't really get into fights. A fight is about saying 'I'm right and I'll beat you until you agree'. The Dutch are more likely to say, 'I'm pretty sure I'm right, but maybe there's something to what you're saying'. It's a lot harder to punch somebody in the teeth when you've got that second thought in your head.

You find this attitude back in almost all of our politics and business as well. The Dutch like to talk, share and compromise. Maybe it's our trader's past. Maybe it has something to do with our protestant roots. I don't know, but what I do know is that this does mean that historically the Dutch are not prone to extremism and generally work hard to find a middle-of-the-road solution for their problems. This even has a name. It's called 'het Poldermodel', which literally refers to low lying land that has been reclaimed from the sea, but in this case is all about consensus building in economics and politics.

By Eddy BERTHIER from Brussels, Belgium [CC BY 2.0], via Wikimedia Commons

Mind you, it doesn't always work out for the best. For example, for a long time Philips, a Dutch company that used to have world-wide brand recognition, was into household electronics, such as radios, VHS recorders, and CD players. The problem was that every single machine they built was a compromise between many different groups and ideas. The resulting machine, rather than being slick, smooth and elegant, ended up being a monstrosity outfitted with so many bells and whistles that it would seem more at home in Frankenstein's laboratory than in your living room. The machines themselves worked well enough, but they had none of that modern day smoothness and designer feel that we've come to expect. And of course you needed an extra box just to fit in the manual! (Okay, that last bit is not actually true). The result? Nowadays Philips is no longer in household electronics. They are still heavily present in medical machinery, however, where function still trumps form.

Also, this trader mentality and over-awareness of egalitarianism does occasionally serve to strip the romance out of a situation. 'Going Dutch', as you may well know, means that everybody in a group pays their own share. In the Netherlands, this will even happen on dates! Similarly, people are often very cerebral and matter-of-fact about relationships. You'll rarely find the stereotypical Mediterranean sense of drama with Dutch partners, with there being very little unreasonable shouting and slamming of doors. Though this is great if you happen to like your eardrums and your doors, sometimes it can be a little unromantic and perhaps even a little cold. Not everything in this world needs to be quite so straightforward.

Another way this egalitarianism shows itself is that in the Dutch switch to a first-name basis almost immediately. Where the Germans go on about 'Herr' this and 'Frau' that, the Dutch will call each other 'Jan' and 'Janneke' right from that start; provided those are their first names of course. We don't just go around calling everybody 'Jan' and 'Janneke'. That would get confusing very quickly!

Interestingly enough, this sense of equality, along with our puritan history, is also why the Dutch don't have any curtains and why the houses are all so similar in design. The reason for this is that you're not supposed to show off. Great wealth, rather than being something to be proud of in classical Dutch society, was something you hid away. For long periods of time the only color that was acceptable for clothing in society was black. And none of that cool, Goth black either, where you get to shave the side of your head and wear eyeliner, no matterwhether you're a man or a woman. No, this was the proper, boring black – the kind worn by Quakers and those that regularly feel a need to cut them self.

Fortunately, we've done away with that dress style. But at least a hint of the need to show you're normal and not extravagant still remains. Obviously the houses in Amsterdam are still as thin as they always were, seeing as the front of most houses are monuments and can't be torn down or modified, but it also shows in our lack of curtains, which is so that the neighbors can look into our houses and make sure we're not doing anything out of the ordinary, like eating off silver plates, or sacrificing babies to Cthulhu. That's also why the Dutch will often say such things as, 'be normal, that's already strange enough' and 'high trees catch a lot of wind', which isn't really about trees, in case you hadn't figured that out.

Dutch liberalism

The Dutch, though still liberal, aren't half as liberal as they used to be, or as they think they are, as has been amply shown by the amount of support the racist politician Geert Wilders has received. This man compared the Quran to 'Mein Kampf' and at one point argued that all people with Moroccan ancestry should be ejected from the country, even if they'd been born here. And yet he still has a (massive) following. Unfortunately, quite a few Dutch people haven't yet clued onto the fact that they aren't quite so liberal. This has led them to saying some very racist things about minority groups, as well as acting all put out when the rest of the world told them the Dutch tradition of depicting the helpers of the Dutch version of Santa Claus as black and stupid, is quite racist. Some people still don't see the racist element in this practice, claiming that it's fine because it is 'tradition'. Maybe somebody should explain to them that when your go-to defense for any activity other people find offensive is 'but its tradition!' you're on the losing side of history.

That said, Amsterdam, with its huge number of different nationalities, is far more liberal than the rest of the country. Here, at least in the city center, gay people can walk hand-in-hand, minorities are safe and not discriminated against, and quite frequently when you start speaking to somebody on the street you'll find they don't speak a word of Dutch. Sometimes this is because they are actually tourists, just in town for a visit. At other times it has do with the fact that forty-five percent of its population has non-Dutch parentage.

In part this is down to the former mayor of Amsterdam, Job Cohen, and his alderman for integration Ahmed Aboutaleb having formulated a policy of "keeping things together" which involves social dialogue, tolerance and harsh measures against those who break the law. To a large extent this has worked, especially in the center of the city and the surrounding districts. The further away from the center you get, however, the greater the social tension does seem to become. Fortunately, most tourists don't make it out that far and so this largely goes unnoticed by the city's visitors.

What the Dutch think of the tourists

In truth, they are kind of ambivalent about them. Though they know they're good for the city's economy, they aren't quite as good for the town itself for several reasons. For one, the tourists seem to be willing to pay outrages prices, which drive up the cost of food and drink in many of the nicer corners of the city center. For another, many tourists seem to think that Amsterdam is some kind of party town, where they can do whatever they want – scream in andacting like idiots in the middle of the night, or walking around without any clothes on – forgetting that the people of Amsterdam still need to get up and go to work in the morning.

I once saw a group of English men on what's known as a 'stag do', or a party to celebrate the fact that one of their friends was getting married. They'd gotten themselves so messed up that they decided to steal a boat and go pleasure cruising. The boat was suitable for maybe four. There were 15 of them. About half way across the canal the boat sank. All fifteen men went under. The police were waiting for them by the canal's side when they came back up again. Though the men in blue are well respected, it isn't that often that they actually get applauded. That day they did, with a whole terrace exploding in spontaneous clapping and cheering as those men got loaded into the back of a police van. We like our boats and we don't like anybody screwing with them.

Of course, the Dutch know that these aren't the only kind of tourists that come to Amsterdam and they're willing to cut many of them – the ones that are respectful – a lot of slack. After all, the city wouldn't be half as beautiful if the tourists didn't come in such large droves to see it. So if you can keep from screaming at 3 A.M., keep from taking your shirt off in the middle of a shopping street and keep remembering that while you're on a vacation, not everybody else is, you'll find the Dutch are very accommodating indeed. What's more, most tourists act like herd animals, going to same squares, the same museums, the same sights and the same streets. As long as the Dutch avoid these, they can avoid the worst of it, which makes the tourists slightly easier to deal with.

Chapter 4: The City Center – beautiful old and touristy

And that is a nice (even if a bit cheeky) lead in to the next part of the guide! The city center is where you'll probably begin your experience of Amsterdam. After all, this is what everybody keeps raving about. Besides, it's probably here that you'll be coming in by train, bus or taxi. Many tourists don't venture out much beyond the center. And there's something to be said for that as well. The outskirts aren't quite as setup for tourists and you do need to know where to go. Also, this is where you find most of the museums, the ancient buildings and the magical streets that you keep seeing in the background of your friends' selfies.

Want to know what is part of the city center and what isn't? Just look for the Singel on any map and you've got most of that line right there. In olden times, this broad canal served both as a highway and a protective moat. Today it serves mainly as an easy marker of where the city center ends and, if you happen to know your way around on a boat, a good way to avoid the frequently overly congested waterways on the city center.

The city center itself is a fantastic combination of narrow streets, canals, cafes, restaurants, as well as confused and exhausted tourists trying to figure out where they are and how the hell they can get back to their hotels. Originally the city actually sat on the two banks of the Amstel River. That part of the river doesn't exist anymore. Its water has been diverted into the canals, creating both more space for buildings and serving as a flushing system to keep the canals far cleaner than most people realize, but you can still see that the city has an 'old' side and a 'new' side. Though both sides are more than antique, they still have a very different vibe to them.

The Dam – shop till you drop

But let's first look at the center of the center, the Dam, which used to be, when the Amstel still flowed through the city, a broad waterway – something you can still see in old images of the city.Now it's one the biggest square, equipped with a rather large phallic symbol (what is it with old cities and their pillars?) The Dam is pretty much exactly at the center of the city and is therefore a useful landmark. Want to get your shop on, or – for that matter – avoid the Amsterdammers? Then this is where to be! There are also often events, like beach volleyball, car shows and fun fairs, on the square itself, as well as huge numbers of street artists, so it's worth checking out.

I would, however, advise against eating or drinking in the restaurants that border the square. They cater almost solely to the tourists that come through and are therefore about twice the price of other locales in the city. Note that in this case expensive does not necessarily mean better. Mind you, possibly things like 'trip advisor' have changed that in the last few years, as suddenly these places have to worry about their reputation, which they didn't need to do before (I honestly don't know, I won't be caught dead in these places). See the chapter 'shopping' for more information about where to go to get your souvenirs, shoes and shopper's sore feet.

The 'old' (eastern) center – the Red Light District and her surroundings

If you head east form the Dam, you'll arrive at the oldest part of the city, which is possibly also the most infamous. Known as 'De Wallen', the 'The Red Light District' to most foreigners and as, 'Whooo yeah! Party!' to the drunken and stoned tourists who only want to see the bottom of beer glasses, the inside of a coffee shop and the space between women's legs, it is actually an incredibly beautiful area of the city. There are big churches, narrow alleyways, old canals and red lit windows filled with dildos, half-naked women and posters advertising sex shows. It is certainly worth a visit, though unless you're of the 'Whooo yeah! Party!' variety, I would advise against it during the evening or on the weekends. I also wouldn't try to use it as a shortcut, as the window shopping men (how often do you see those three words together?) are so numerous you could probably crowd surf the entire area if you were so inclined and didn't mind the possibility of being dumped in a canal.

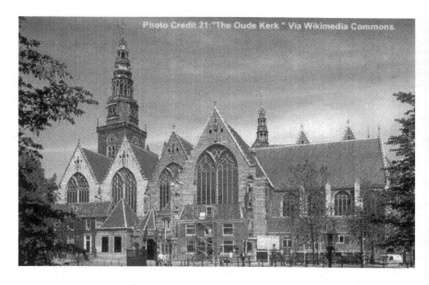
Photo Credit 21: "The Oude Kerk " Via Wikimedia Commons

A warning: This area is a little more dangerous than most, in that pickpockets sometimes still operate here, so if you do decide to go for a wander, make sure to keep your purses closed and your hands on your pockets. Still, it's not half as bad as you might have been led to believe. There are plenty of police patrols and surveillance cameras.

Why would you want to use the red light district as a short cut, you ask? Well, there are actually some really nice areas surrounding it. To the north east there's the Nieuwemarkt, which is big square lined with cafes, coffeeshops and eateries. It is dominated by the hulking presence of 'De Waag', or the weighing house, where the merchants went in yea olden days to get their scales properly balanced and their weights approved, something that was necessary as there was no global standardization, no metric system and no super accurate electronic scales for sale in the nearest corner shop, for that matter. The Nieuwemarkt is a great place to go on a weekend (which includes Thursday night, student night), as there's a good mix of tourists and locals here. To the north east there's the

Zeedijk, which runs from the Nieuwemarktto Centraal station and is also the seat of city's tiny China town (though really it should be called 'Asian town'), where there are some very affordable and tasty eateries.

Photo Credit 20:"De Wallen red-light district" by Rungbachduong Licensed under CC BY-SA 3.0 via Wikimedia Commons

On the south southern edge of the Red Light district, runs the Damstraat, which starts at the Dam and shoots off to the east. It isn't actually all that great, but does have some descent restaurants, including a two-story Asian place called Oriental City that does pretty decent dim sum – be warned though, on weekends the line can be long. I've had to wait for an hour once or twice.

Be careful on the Damstraat itself! As the sidewalks are very crowdedyou might be tempted to step onto the actual street to get past somebody. Watch out when you do so, as it's a major route for the Dutch to get from east to west and vice versa. As they're generally in a hurry, they come through this street at speed on their bicycles.A lot of tourists that have just arrived in Amsterdam wander down this street, not realizing that unlike back home where most vehicles are motorized bicycles don't make any sound, and step onto the street without looking behind them. I wouldn't be surprised if this street is where the most accidents happen in the entire city. It certainly is where you'll see the most enraged Dutch people screaming obscenities at very surprised tourists.

From the Nieuwemarktyou can head south, along the Kloveniersburgwal, which is a beautiful little canal with diversions on both sides of the water. Look for churches, chapels, attractive canals, and some notable historic buildings, which the University of Amsterdam owns and where a lot of students go to ignore the architecture and instead put their heads in books. At the end you'll find the Amstel and a wonderful terrace deck that juts out into the water, where you can sit and watch the boats go by.

Farthest west, running parallel to the Rokin, is the Nes theater district, while if you head east, you'll find the Old Jewish Quarter, which includes the synagogue complex of the JoodsHistorischMuseum. It's worth a visit, as until the Second World War the Jewish population of Amsterdam played a vital role in the city (see 'the city's history' for more on this). It wouldn't be much of an exaggeration, in fact, to say that Amsterdam was what Jerusalem is today (minus the religious significance). In fact, one of the colloquial names for the city, 'Mokkum' means 'the Place' in Hebrew. This is not the only Hebrew word to have snuck into Amsterdam vocabulary either, with such words as 'mazzel' and 'smeris' (luck and police, respectively) still being used today.

Onwards to the Western part of the center!

The 'New' Center – the Grachtengordel, de Jordaan, het Leidseplein and the NegenStraatjes

What's that word, you ask? Grachtengordel? Which crazy lunatic thought it would be a good idea to put those letters together? I have no idea, but it was a Dutch lunatic, that's for sure (Just for fun, when you get to Amsterdam, get a local to teach you how to say that word. It's wonderful for clearing the sinuses). The word means 'Canal Belt' and runs from the Amstel River to the Brouwersgracht (Brewers' canal), with four big canals – which look like they're spooning each other on the map – running from the South-East to the West. This famous district was built in 17th-century and the whole area is a designated UNESCO World

Heritage Site for its unique cultural and historical value. This place is expensive. To rent a house here is going to sink your budget faster than the city itself is disappearing into the muck. Yes, that's right, the city was built on a swamp and is sinking into the mud. So hurry up and go and see it before it's all gone! (No need to panic, you've got a few centuries).

The New Center is probably what you've seen all the pictures of, with the sun setting between the trees along those beautiful wide canals. It truly is absolutely gorgeous, with its lattice of olive-green waterways and dinky humpback bridges overlooked by street upon street of handsome seventeenth-century canal houses, undisturbed by later architectural developments. It's a subtle cityscape full of surprises, with a bizarre carving here and an unusual facade there. Architectural peccadilloes aside, it is the district's overall atmosphere that appeals rather than any specific sight. Really, the best way to tackle the area is just to wander for a while, as every street is as interesting as the last.

One definite advantage is thatin the Grachtengordel itself there aren't that many shops, nor is it that crowded, and so you can wander along, staring upwards, without having to worry that you'll trip over somebody. Sometimes, even in the middle of summerwhen the people are the thickest on the ground, you can wander down one of the canals with not a person in sight and for a few minutesand let your imagination wing free, pretending that you're right back in the 17th century itself (provided you can ignore the cars).

The northern area of the Grachtengordelis called 'de Jordaan' (pronounced Yore-dahn). Although this cozy, scenic, and singular neighborhood's working-class roots have long since withered, it remains an area rich in picturesque canals and historic courtyards – a wanderer's paradise.While this once-poor district has had one of the city's most colorful histories, today the Jordaanis most certainly upmarket. Its 1895 population of 80,000, which made it one of the densest in Europe, has declined to a mere 14,000. But in many ways, the Jordaan will always remain the Jordaan, even though its narrow alleys and leafy canals are now lined with quirky specialty shops, restaurants, galleries, and designer boutiques, especially along the NegenStraatjes, or the nine streets.

This rather unimaginatively named area of the town consists of nine parallel streets that start with the Reestraat (roe deer street) and end with the WijdeHeistraat (wide heath street). Don't let rather uninspiring naming fool you, however, for this is a very artistic and hip (can we still use that word in a positive manner?) area of town, with wonderful little restaurants, cafes and specialty shops. Though it's certainly full of tourists, here the number of locals start to rival the tourists– though obviously, with it being in the center and the shops being cool and swanky, they are a certain well-heeled kind of local.

Photo Credit 23 "Prinsengracht" by Diliff
Licensed under CC BY 2.5 via Wikimedia Commons

In the olden days this area wasn't at all desirable. For example, many of these streets were named after the animal skin tanning that went on there. And in case you're not familiar with medieval tanning, it was a dirty and above all very stinky process, not just because of the flecks of meat that would scraped off the skins and left to rot, but mainly because in medieval times they would often use urine and dog feces to treat the skins. Naturally, this reflected poorly on the surrounding area and meant that what is now one of the most expensive parts of town, back then was among its poorest. Living conditions were overcrowded and squalid, and the inhabitants gained a reputation for rebelliousness.

Another important landmark in this area is the 'Leidseplein'. This square is famous for its nightlife and the clubs that surround it, the street performances on it and the fact that from the city center it is the gateway to the Vondelpark, Amsterdam's most famous park (which is covered more extensively under 'west to the vondelpark' a few pages on). The square can be found in the south west of the city, right on the outskirts of the city center. In truth, this square is almost as touristy as the Dam, something that you can't help but notice when you try to buy something in any of the bars or cafes bordering it (You want how much for a beer? Are you nuts? In most countries, I could get a hip replacement for that much money!) Fortunately, there are a lot of areas around the square that aren't that expensive.To get a feel for where to go after the sun sets, check out the 'nightlife' section.

Two beautiful bridges– The skinny bridge and the Staalmeestersbrug

Though many of the bridges in the center are beautiful, two in particular are worth visiting. The first is the Skinny Bridge, which leaps the Amstelbetween Keizersgracht and Prinsengracht. If you've seen more than a handful of pictures of the city of Amsterdam, you've probably seen this bridge as well. In the past, it used to be lit up with halogen lightbulbs and the truth is, that was actually far more beautiful. Still, the modern LED lights are more environmentally friendly, and since Amsterdam is one of the cities at risk of flooding when the sea levels rise, there's something to be said for them being as green as possible.

The second bridge worth visiting is the Staalmeestersbrug (or the steel masters' bridge). Though the bridge itself is not as impressive as the Magerebrug, the view north, along the canal, lined with beautiful trees and completed with a view of the Zuidertoren (Southern tower) at its end, is truly spectacular. Apparently, I'm not the only one who thinks so, as tourists and locals alike have started hanging countless locks to pronounce their undying love all over the bridge. It is now apparently too heavy to raiseand the city has threatened to cut the locks off, but so far has not actually done so. We can only hope they hold off as long as possible.

Bijgenhof and a free look in the Amsterdam Historical Museum

Two more sights that are certainly worth it are the Bijgenhof and the free gallery in the Amsterdam Historical Museum, which are located conveniently close together. The Begijnhof, which can be hard to find as it's hidden behind two nondescript wooden doors, is one of the city's best known hofjes (almshouses). The little square, just off the Spui, is lined with historic buildings, mostly private dwellings and a little church. It dates back from the early 14th century, when it was built to offer safety to single catholic women, the Begijntjes, in a time when such women had few opportunities. These women, though they took no monastic vows, in effect lived like nuns in the heart of the city. The square is absolutely beautiful, tranquil (you can't hear the sounds of the city itself at all) and the atmosphere seems almost sanctified.

Amsterdam's oldest surviving house 'Het Houten Huis' (the wooden house), dating from around 1420, is located there. On the adjoining walls, there is a fascinating collection of wall plaques with biblical themes. The southern fringe of the square is dominated by the EngelseKerk (English Church) which dates from the 15th century and possesses its original medieval tower. The Begijnhof Chapel, a clandestine catholic church in a protestant city, was completed in 1680. It contains many reminders of the Catholic past. Houses in Begijnhof are still occupied by single women, so you should respect their privacy.Note that though you can wander in on your own, tour groups are not allowed inside.

Close by is a free exhibit of the Amsterdam Historical Museum, which consists of an impressive gallery of old portraits of the important citizens of Amsterdam displayed in a high, naturally lit corridor. These things are big and impressive, showing some of the leading citizens of the city during those times (why don't we do that kind of thing anymore? Is it because we can't even hold still long enough even for selfies, let alone three weeks of painting?)

The Civic Guards Gallery (Schuttersgalerij), as the place is called, is accessible to all visitors from the Begijnhof via a huge glass entryway, located at the far end of the courtyard. To get there, leave the Begijnhof and immediately take a left to the GedempteBegijneslootstreet. It is a dead end, but you'll find a glass doors at the end. Though there is a guard, he won't stop you, provided you are appropriately attired and aren't wielding a water pistol, a katana, or anything else that might damage the paintings.

Chapter 5: Outside of the center and away from the tourists

Everybody always says that Amsterdam is an old city – and that's true, to an extent. The thing is, it's only the city center that's truly ancient. The rest of the city was only built in the 19th century, when the industrial revolution took the cute little place and turned into a metropolis (okay, maybe 'metropolis' is an overstatement, global village is probably more accurate). Don't let this make you think that the city center is the only place worth seeing, however. Yes, that's where most of the sight you've heard about are, but that doesn't mean the rest isn't worth it. There are interesting architectural innovations, like the Westerdok, to the west of Centraal station, and then there are parks, and markets to boot. What's more – and possibly more importantly – it is in the outskirts that you're really going to see how the Dutch live and love.

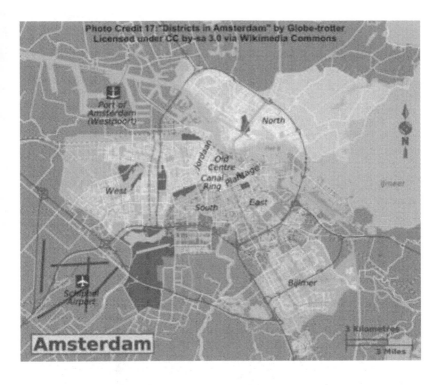

West to the Vondelpark

Though all the parks in Amsterdam are pretty and important, the Vondelpark, with its 10 million annual visitors, sticks out head and shoulders above the rest. It is undoubtedly the city's back garden (which is important in a city where most people live in apartments). This is where the vast majority of the people go on the more beautiful days of summer to hang out and have fun, with the younger people and the tourists congregating more near the front of the park, while the crowd gets both older, quieter, more relaxed and more local the further back you go. And you can go a long way back indeed, as the 45 hectares that make up the park are stretched out in a long, thin rectangular shape. This means you can walk a good thirty minutes without leaving the park – impressive for such a dense city, no?

Photo Credit 46 "Vondelpark" by Fakpek Licensed under Public Domain via Wikimedia Commons

It is located south of Leidseplein and near Rijksmuseum, Stedelijk Museum and Van Gogh Museum and on a sunny day the place often seems more like a festival than a city park, with people jogging, roller skating, barbequing, making music, practicing acrobatics, picnicking and more down its entire length. Free concerts are frequently given at the open-air theatre or at the park's bandstand. You'll find the schedule for what's going on when online. Other attractions are the statue of the poet Vondel, the cast iron music dome, the Groot Melkhuis(milk house) which has a playground for children, the historical Pavilion with its restaurant Vertigo, and het Blauwe thee huis (the Blue Tea House), which has seating outside both upstairs and downstairs.

The park has been around for a long time. In 1864 a group of prominent citizens formed a committee to found a public park. They raised money to buy eight hectares of land and the landscape architect Jan David Zocher was commissioned to design the park in a fashionable English landscape style. Zocher worked with his son Louis Paul Zocher. The two were trained in Paris and Rome, and had learned to use vistas, ponds and pathways to create an illusion of natural areas.

The park was opened to public in 1865 as a horseback riding and strolling park named 'Nieuwe Park'. The name Vondelpark was adopted in 1867 when a statue of Dutch poet Joost van den Vondel was put up. More money was soon raised and the park was enlarged in 1877 to its current size. At that time, it was located on the edge of Amsterdam, since then the city has grown to swallow it up in its entirety.

Constructed on a muddy dump area, the Vondelpark has to be renovated in its entirety every 30 years. This is because the park is constantly sinking, which means that sooner or later they'd have to start calling it the Vondel lake and barbequing there would be far more challenging. As pumping out the ground water would damage the surrounding buildings, they have to raise the park instead.

The park has many old plane trees, horse chestnut, Dutch red chestnut, catalpas and different sorts of birch trees. Numerous bushes and herbs complete the park's landscape. Vondelpark is also home to many birds – wild ducks, blue herons and other birds. Some of the rarer bird kinds even have their own areas, where unauthorized people are not permitted to go.

South to the AlbertcuypMarktthe Amstel park and the Amsterdamsebos

Though the Waterlooplein market might be the one all the tourists know about, the Albertcuyp market is actually far better and more authentically Dutch. Where the first has been completely filled up with crap for tourists, in the latter you can still get real Dutch food, such as cheese, paling, or raw fish, and freshly baked stroopwafels (translates as 'syrup waffles', which are better than Dutch pancakes when they're freshly baked– yes, I just went there). The market also feels far more like an actual market, with people calling out what they've got on offer in thick Amsterdam accents and the prices on perishables steadily falling as the day wears on. Also, though there are obviously going to be tourists, this really still feels like Dutch Amsterdam, with the place primarily populated by locals. Note that the market is closed on Sunday.

Around the streetand, in fact, throughout the Pijp (Pipe) as the area is called, there are lots of cool little bars, where you can have a drink or a meal at a far more reasonable price than back in the center. As with the market, this area is also populated mainly by locals and expats (which in Amsterdam are pretty much one and the same).

This area is quickly being gentrified, but hasn't quite got there yet. This area was pulled out of the ground to house workers, something that's easy to notice if you look at the houses, which are much simpler and more straightforward in their design. They are also much smaller than what you'll find in the center. Originally, it was actually envisioned by the first person commissioned to design it, Mr. Saphati, as an area that would have wide boulevards and big parks, much in the spirit of Paris. The city council rejected his ideas, however, and instead chose for a design that featured much smaller streets and parks. All Saphati got for his trouble was a park named after him. Ironically, it's a rather small park.

A much bigger park is the Amstel park. This baby is a bit of a distance outside of the center, but if you like parks, it's well worth the trip, It has numerous beautiful gardens, various attractions for children, a café, a restaurant, two galleries and mini-golf course (and who doesn't love the frustration of hitting the blades of that damned windmills for the third time in a row?) The park was established in 1972. And it is, as the name suggests, located along the Amstel river, which makes for a spectacular view. The park contains a rhododendron valley with 139 sorts of the plant (8000 bushes, some of them four meters high), the Rosarium (a rose garden), a Belgium cloister garden, a butterfly friendly garden and more.

Near the Amstel park there's the Rieker windmill, which was built all the way back in 1636, which – as you might remember – wasn't all that long after Amsterdam received its city rights. Just behind the windmill, there is a small bronze monument to Rembrandt, as the story goes that this was one of his favorite walking routes, which apparently influenced his prints. Continue on, further along the river bank, in a southerly direction, and you'll eventually reach the small village of Oudekerk. It is well worththe visit, as it will give you a good sense of what life was like in the Dutch countryside – plus it's amazingly pretty, with the village embodying many Dutch rural building styles.

But let's head back into town and head for the AmsterdamseBos, or Amsterdam forest. This park didn't start out as a forest, instead it was constructed on unused turf lands and wetlands just outside the city (yes, pretty much everything in Amsterdam was constructed!), but you wouldn't know that by looking at it today. There is one advantage to its artificiality and that is that since everything has been planned and arranged and so it has numerous sports and leisure facilities. For example, there is a long thin lake, that's meant for rowing and other areas specifically meant other kinds of watersports. The big attraction in winter is De Heuvel (The Hill) - an artificial mountain with one slope left free of growth, so that when it does snow, children can go sledding and skiing down it.Artificiality – better than reality! Well, at least in Amsterdam that's true.

The Bos is a marvelous place where you can relax walking, bicycling, go picnicking, canoeing and – on those few days of the year the weather permits – skiing. The size of the park is comparable in its size to Bois de Boulogne in Paris and it has the feel of the

English countryside, in that it giving its visitor an unrestricted view out across the landscape. It was built on a specially created polder 13 feet (4 meters) below sea level. The park opened in 1937 and was expanded to its current size in 1964. Of course, it hasn't been static, with the place constantly undergoing renovations and improvements throughout its almost eighty years of existence.

By the main entrance you will see two big bunker-like constructions, one on either side of the road. The one on the right is a nice, big café with a huge terrace, where you can sit anytime the weather is nice, while the one on the left is the visitor's center, which includes a reception area, a souvenir shop and an exhibition center which explains the park's history.

Photo Credit 49: "Amsterdamse Bos" by Shirley de Jong
Licensed under CC BY-SA 3.0 via Wikimedia Commons

One more area that requires special mention is the open-aired theatre, built in the summer of 1985. The stage is set out in front of a large grassy amphitheater, which is just a perfect place to relax with a blanket, some snacks and a bottle (or two) of wine. The entire stage is surrounded by forest. I couldn't imagine a better place to watch something like Shakespeare's A Midsummer Night's Dream, could you?

East to the Amsterdam ZOO and the Botanical gardens

Amsterdam boasts the oldest zoo in the Netherlands. Artis, as it's called, is close to the heart of the city andis a joy to visit, with over 900 types of animals, as well as 200 types of trees. What's more, there is some wonderful 19th century architecture to admire, with there being numerous listed buildings on the grounds, like the Large Museum (1855), the unique Library building (1867) and the Aquarium (1882). If the price, at €19.50 per adult, is a little high, however, then there is another option, which is to float by. A large part of Artist borders the water and though a lot of it is walled off, there are some sections where you can see inside. On the many cruises I've taken past it, I've seen giraffes, zebras and even been followed by odd looking birds who might have mistaken our boat for their mother (it was also an odd looking boat). I've been told that the canals around the zoo are inhabited with turtles, which come out to sun themselves on the nice days. Unfortunately, I've never been lucky enough to see them.

The HortusBotanicus is the world's oldest botanical garden and the reason it was built is fascinating. You see, before the reformation there were numerous catholic monasteries in and around the city. When the city became protestant, however, these were all closed and their land and riches confiscated. This created a bit of a problem, as suddenly the city lost its access the herbs and spices that the monks used to grow and the pharmacists and doctors had used in their healing practices. The HortusBotanicus was the solution and in effect it started off as a glorified herb garden. Of course, today it is far more than that.

The glass walls of the Hortusserve as a giant green house, which allows the building to house three different tropical climates – quite an achievement when you consider the Dutch weather. Through this process the building is able to house more than 6000 different plants. Some of which are unique, like, for example, the 2000-year-old agave cactus and a 300-year-old Eastern Kape giant cycad. There are two different suggested routes to go through the place, one that gives an evolutionary perspective, while the other allows you to see the 24 big trees inside. Another possibility is to go inside to get away from the Dutch weather and hang out in the agreeable warmth. If that's why you're going there, might I suggest the beautiful café, located in the recently renovated Orangery, which has a large 'outside' terrace? The garden is a five minute walk away from the Rembrandts House and close to Artis – Amsterdam ZOO, as well as the Resistance Museum.

North, across the water, to villages in the city

The North, which is only a free ferry ride away, is fascinating, in that large parts have only recently been built up and therefore not completely integrated. This creates a fascinating clash of styles. True, large parts of it are boring blocky architecture that's more at home in other cities, like flats and such, but if you know where to go, then you'll suddenly chance upon streets that are throwbacks to the villages that used to dot the area, back before the tunnels and the ferries made transportation to and from here as easy as it is today.

One particular road I heartily advice is the Nieuwdammerdijk (or the new Amsterdam dike), which is only 'new' in the sense that most things in Amsterdam are 'new'. The village, which stretches along the dike, was originally incorporated into Amsterdam in 1921, but has barely been modified away from its original architecture. Most of the houses are tiny one story affairs, with thatch roofs. There is a village bar and a hand operated lock. The place seems like it's been taken straight out of a history book. Keep going along it and you'll find yourself in the Dutch countryside. Well worth a go if you've got bicycles (and a bit of stamina).

Chapter 6: Transportation – cars, bikes, trams, busses, boats and the trusty foot wagon

There are many ways of getting around Amsterdam. You can opt for the bike, trams, busses, taxi or the ever-trusty blobs at the end of your legs (did you know that the human feet contains 52 bones, which is equivalent to 25% of the bones in your body? Crazy, right? No wonder the bastards hurt so much when you kick something on the way to the refrigerator late at night!)

Step by step

Amsterdam, especially in the center, is an exceedingly walkable city. If you know your way around, or are good at reading maps, everything within the city center is only half hour's brisk walk away at most. If you're trying to see the big tourist's attractions, there are actually signs pointing them out. For everywhere else, you've got to have a good sense of direction and a good memory, or an app, to deal with the city's crooked streets (see 'short cuts and how not to get lost').

What is more, though walking is obviously slower than bicycling, it has the big advantage that you can take your time and look around. When you're riding through town on two wheels, there is a lot to keep track of, like keeping your balance, other bicyclists and traffic in general. Though walking still requires some attention, the slower pace means you've got more time to gaze up at the beautiful ancient buildings that line every street – heck, one street in the center of Amsterdam probably has more history than some counties! There really is something to see in every street and as long as you don't allow yourself to get too consumed with arriving and instead are able to enjoy the actual process of approaching, you will never run out of things to see.

At one point, for about half a year, I decided I didn't want to bike any more, and walked everywhere, so that I could really enjoy this city that I called home. I lived in the center and this was very doable – though occasionally my friends thought otherwise. It was also great for my calves. One important note! The streets in Amsterdam are often cobbled. This is really beautiful, but doesn't work with heels at all. Therefore, if you're planning to do any walking, make sure you wear flats! Don't believe me? Check out the Dutch women's foot wear. Believe them. They're not just doing it because they're tall.

Bicycles – organized chaos on two (million) wheels

The bicycle is the Amsterdamer's metal steed. It is their freedom, their liberty and their transportation to work and party to boot. Apparently 40% of the people in Amsterdam go to work on their bike and there are 400 kilometers of bike paths. In truth, that doesn't do the amount of bicycle traffic in the city justice, as those that don't take bicycle are much more likely to live on the city's outskirts, where driving is actually possible, while the center is really at its most accessible on the back of one of these metal tightrope acts.

The city sure is designed for it. Everywhere you go you'll see bike lanes, bike racks and, of course, the bikes themselves, whether with (several) somebody(s) on their back, or chained with several locks to whatever object looks convenient and not likely to go anywhere soon (note that draw bridges are not good places to chain your bikes). Those locks are essential, because unfortunately there is a propensity in the city for bicycles to go 'missing'. This has been a massive problem from the seventies onwards. Fortunately, recently it has been getting a bit better. The reason is that in the past there was a large addict population in the city, who would steal bicycles and then sell them for the equivalent of 5 Euros, so as to get their next fix.

There was a time in the sixties where Amsterdam tried this innovative thing called the 'white bike plan', where they offered free white bicycles to everybody in the city, under the guidelines that they should put them back when they were done with them. Most people did. Unfortunately, most is not enough and a few rotten apples spoiled the apple barrel, as they say. More and more of the bicycles disappeared and eventually the plan was abandoned. To be replaced with what the locals came to know as the black bicycle plan, which was where the junkies stole everybody's bikes and you got so frustrated that you paid them the damned five Euros, just to get a 'new' bicycle. Of course, you knew it was illegal, you knew it was wrong, but you also knew that buying yet another legal bike (the sixth one that year) was going to put you back another 50 Euros and that was becoming a more expensive habit than that of the junkies hunting their next fix.

Fortunately, that's not so much a problem anymore. In part that's because the local government made it a crime to buy such bicycles (the junkies themselves didn't care very much about selling them, as the offences were always too minor for them to go to jail for any length of time and they never paid the fines). Probably more importantly, the government also supplied the junkies with free methadone (a heroine substitute) and heroin use has been declining steadily over the last few decades. Still, lock your bikes. The bike rental companies do not take kindly to you sheepishly telling them that you don't have their property anymore. You can also use guarded bicycle parking stations (Fietsenstalling) for a nominal fee.

There is one phenomenal one near to the main train station which is actually multiple stories!

Photo Credit 10: "Parking at Fietsflat near Centraal Station" by Luu Licensed under Public Domain via Wikimedia Commons

When do decide to get on a bike, don't smoke a joint first! For some reasons a lot of tourists seem to think that this is a good idea. It is not. Biking in Amsterdam means paying attention to a lot of factors, not just which way the pedals go and how to keep your steer straight. You need to watch the other bicyclists, the cars, the streets and the rails of the tram. That last one is very, very important. I'm not kidding. Your bike wheels are just thin enough to slip easily into that metal dip. When that happens your bike will suddenly be jerked sideways and only with a great deal of experience and luck will you be able to yank it back out again. If you don't, well, then you get to say hello to the Dutch cobble stones. And that is a meeting you won't soon forget. If you're aware of the danger, you can steer across them pretty easily. The trick is to make sure you don't try to cross them too diagonally. If you hit them at close to a right angle, they aren't dangerous; it's when you hit them at a slant that you get into trouble.

Also, Dutch bicyclists don't follow the rules. Though they are basically supposed to follow the same ones as the cars, they really don't. They will pass on the left and on the right, they will take red traffic lights as suggestions, and they will go the wrong way down a one way street. You've got to be prepared for this. When you first throw yourself out there, it can seem like complete madness. It is, in fact, a study in social civility, with people minding each other instead of the rules, to make sure there are as few collisions as possible. And you'll find there are surprisingly few of them.

Except if you're a stoned idiot tourist, of course, who is completely unaware both of how things work and anything ten degrees to the left or the right of what's straight ahead of them, for that matter. Fortunately, the tourist bikes are vivid colors, so that the locals are aware that the people on them might not be completely aware of how things work. At the same time, there is only so much you can do as a local if a tourist suddenly decides to make a right turn without first looking if there's somebody there.

Don't let all that discourage you. If you've got some bicycling experience, you'll probably be fine. Just stick to the bike paths (they are brown), don't stop or turn suddenly and when you do need to stop, first angle for the right side and get near the foot path. Also, look over your shoulder when you go left or right! This isn't just to make you aware of whose there, but also to make those who are there aware of what you're planning to do. That's what I was talking about when spoke about social civility. And even if you do have a collision, it will be at low speeds and you'll probably walk away with a few bruises or scratches; except if you get caught in one of those tram rails of course. That really is a horrible way to crash. Oh yes and watch out for trams themselves.

Also note that when you see a big blue pedestrian sign, that counts for bicycles as well. And this is one of the rules that the Dutch police do enforce, as if they didn't these areas would become bike paths within a matter of days (and it is no fun for anybody when bicyclists start weaving through a crowd of pedestrians). Also, at night you need lights. The police will have random spot checks to see if you have them, and obviously they have a pretty easy time seeing when you don't. Though I might have said that the Dutch police are very civil, not having lights is not one of those things you'll be able to talk your way out of. Believe me, I've tried.

Want to explore the countryside a little bit? If you're in relatively good condition, the bike is the way to go. Within half an hour you're out of town. You can go north, take the ferry across the IJ to Waterland. Or go south, into the AmsterdamseBos (see the entry about it in 'South to the AlbertcuypMarkt the Amstel park and the Amsterdamsebos'). You can also follow the river Amstel where Rembrandt worked or take your bike on the metro to the end of the line at Gaasperplas, and cycle along rivers and windmills to old fortified towns like Weesp, Muiden and Naarden.

Sold? Great, here's how you get one of these wonderful metal contraptions! There are bike rental shops at the bigger stations, and several others in and around the city center. Bikes cost about €9 to €20 per day. If they offer you a standard bike, or one with gears, take a standard one! They are far more robust and really the only time you ever need gears is with the bridges – the rest of Amsterdam is as flat as a Dutch pancakes. What's more, gears just mean there's an extra thing to think about, when there's already so much going on! On the other hand, hand brakes (the ones on the steer) are probably better for the inexperienced bicyclist than back kick brakes (the ones in the pedals), as the latter take some getting used to.

Public transportation – or how to get around without getting rained on

The trams, busses and metros in the Netherlands are well organized and easy to use, provided you have what's known as an OV-chipkaart, as a few years ago the old ticket system was abandoned in the name of progress. This is something everybody has regretted since. Oh well, since we can't turn back the clock, you can get one from GVB vending machines at all metro stations, from the desks at some bigger stations (including Centraal Station) and some shops. In the stations there are generally some people standing around in uniforms that can help you. Their uniforms say GVB. If their uniforms say something else, like McDonalds, they might not be quite as knowledgeable (though you might be able to get fries with that).

To use the cards, tap them onto the reader when you enter and exit the tram. If everything is in order and you have enough money, the reader will make a jolly little 'boop' sound. If there aren't sufficient funds, some other card in your wallet is interfering, or you're trying to check in with your Starbucks card, you'll hear multiple angry beeps. It is fine, at this point, to mutter angrily about the state of affairs these days, how nostalgia ain't what it used to be and try again. If it continues to beep angrily, then it's probably time to top up your card (you need a minimum of €4 on your card for the tram or bus and €20 for the train). You can't do that on the bus or the tram (because that would be logical). You'll have to go to a metro station or a train station. You can buy a one-hour or 24-hour card in the bus or tram. Remember to check out when you exit the vehicle! Otherwise a two-stop trip will get very expensive as you'll be charged €4 euros (€20 on the train).

There are three types of OV-chipkaarten; a personal card on which you can load weekly/monthly/yearly subscriptions, an anonymous card on which you can load money, and a disposable card which can be used for a limited number of hours. The first two types cost €7.50 for the card and you have to have at least €4 on it to be able to travel on trams and busses (€20 on the train).

For visitors, the most useful type of travel pass is probably the 1/24/48/72/96/120/144/168 hour tickets, issued as a disposable OV-card, with no base fee. This allows the holder to travel on an unlimited number of journeys on tram, metro and GVB bus services throughout that period. On a tram, only the 1 and 24 hour tickets can be purchased. These passes are also available at tourist offices located at Schiphol airport and just outside Centraal Station, many hotels and GVB Tickets & Infooffices. Note that day passes are not valid on buses operated by Connexxion and Arriva. If you plan to stay longer in Amsterdam, you can buy discounted weekly or monthly tickets from most post offices or other ticket sale points. These are more affordable.

Disposable GVB tickets are not valid on trains to Schiphol airport, as there is a surcharge, but you can use them on buses to Schiphol. For tourists that plan to visit a lot of museums and sights, the "I AMsterdam City Card" might be the best option. It gives free entrance to some museums and attractions (and discounts on others), unlimited public transport operated by GVB in Amsterdam, discounts, free giveaways and special offers. You can use this card outside of Amsterdam, too. The museums element of your card is automatically activated the first time you visit a museum or attraction, while the public transport element is activated the first time you use a tram, bus or metro. Once activated, each element remains valid for 24, 48 or 72 hours, depending on the type of card you got. The price for 24 hours is €49, the price for 48 hours is €59, and the I AMsterdam City Card for 72 hours costs €69.

Public transport within the city is operated by the GVB. The main way to get around is with the trams, which go almost everywhere. There are also dozens of night bus routes which run in place of the trams between midnight and 5 am. All tram stops have detailed mapsof the routes and the surrounding area. Admittedly they are a little complicated. You can also get a free public transport map at the GVB Tickets & Info offices, or in the tram. Most trams have conductors, near the back. If you don't have a ticket, you can get one from the driver or the conductor. Just remember that here you can only buy the one hour and 24hour tickets. Almost everyone speaks English, so don't hesitate to ask if you're lost, aren't sure the tram goes in the right direction or don't understand something.

All trams have pre-recorded audio announcements indicating the next stop, with most also having automated displays. All stations are announced in Dutch, while those where a lot of tourists want to go are announced in English as well, along with the attractions that are there. Handy, right?

Besides the tram, there is also a four-line metro, while they're still busy building the fifth, which is supposed to be done in 2017 (well it was supposed to be done ages ago, but you know how it is). The four lines all start at central station and head out from there.

By Mauritsvink (Own work) [Public domain], via Wikimedia Commons

There are also intercity buses to nearby towns such as Haarlem and Uithoorn; these are operated by Connexxion or EBS and can be used within Amsterdam if you travel with an OVchipkaart. Disposable cards cannot be used, as they are only valid on the GVB buses. All the bus lines and routes are available online or at stops. There are also some helpful apps available for smartphone users, where you can put in where you are and where you want to go and the app will do the rest (left foot, right foot).

Getting across the IJ

There are several free ferry services across the IJ (aye) River, from Central station to Amsterdam North. They are all free. The most frequent one runs every 7 min. They all leave from a new jetty on the northern (rear) side of Centraal Station, with two heading pretty much straight across, while the third one heads off to the NDSM Werf, which is a funky up-and-coming industrial neighborhood with a few bars and restaurants. Ferries to the werf leave every 30 minutes from Centraal Station during normal hours, while they double in frequency during peak hours (as they do on all the ferry lines).

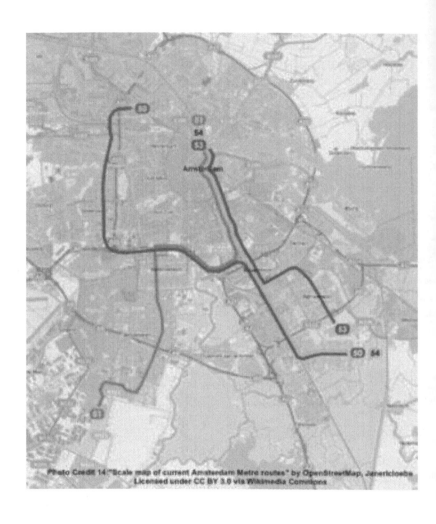

Photo Credit 14:"Scale map of current Amsterdam Metro routes" by OpenStreetMap, Jenericbloebe. Licensed under CC BY 3.0 via Wikimedia Commons

Do note that only one of the ferries, the ferry to Buiksloterweg (yes, that's a place)goes all night! The other ones all stop in the evening, with the one going straight across to IJplein stopping ten minutes to midnight, while the one that goes to the NDSM werfstopping at midnight. This can be quite a bother, especially as you're at the NDSM werf, as it's quite a trek back to the ferry that does run. So pay attention to the time!

By Boat – the Canals of Amsterdam

Though traveling through Amsterdam on a bicycle might be the way that everybody says you've got to see the city, doing it by boat is – in fact – much nicer. Where getting on the back of a bike means dodging traffic, avoiding collisions and working at not falling over, none of these problems present themselves on the boats (okay, you might have to work at not falling over after a couple of drinks, but that's not quite the same thing). The easiest way to see the canals by boat is to go with one of the big companies, like Holland International, Canal, Blue Boat, RederijKooij, RederijPlas and Lovers, which offer a safe ride and a consistent level of quality. At the same time, they don't exactly make you feel special – more like sardines in a transparent can, if you ask me.

Photo Credit 15: "Tourist boat Amsterdam" by Vitaly Volkov Licensed under CC BY 2.5 via Wikimedia Commons

If you want something different, then get onto one of the smaller boats. There's two ways to do this, you can either rent one and steer it around yourself, or hire a boat with a skipper. Don't have any experience with boats? I highly recommend the latter, because the canals of Amsterdam are not the right place to learn, especially on sunny days where there are more boats then there is water. Yes, the boat you rent are sturdy and not likely to sink, but this is not the case for many of the other boats cruising through the canals and, speaking from personal experience, having a ham-fisted tourist ram one of these battering-ram like contraptions into the side of your boat can ruin your day (and lead to a lot of paper work). Still want to do it yourself? Well, then there are several rental companies in Amsterdam that will pop up if you do an online search. They will provide you with a boat, personal instruction and a good map before you leave. The boats are electric and straightforward to steer.

To pursue the other option, you need to find smaller operators, which are also online. These offer boats, as well as captains who will take care of the actual steering, so that you can relax and enjoy the view. These boats are far more comfortable than the tubs you steer yourself and equipped with a great deal more amenities. Quite often these captains also operate as guides and know a lot of interesting information about the city. Many of these services provide drinks, food and cover against the rain that can show up at any time in Amsterdam. Others allow you to bring your own food and drink onboard. Make sure you enquire before you get on. Also, the price ranges differ considerably, so spend a bit of time doing some research.

Taxis – expensive, just like everywhere else

About 15 years ago, after the taxi market was liberalized and the monopoly position of the main company cracked wide open, there was a taxi war across all of the Netherlands. And with that I don't mean a price war, or a service war. I mean an actual war. One incident I remember reading about was when a group of taxis blocked off the escape of a competitor's cab and proceeded to light it on fire, while the taxi driver and his customers were still inside it! Other incidents included such things as pitched battles at taxi stands, where groups attacked competitors and their cabs with fists, clubs, bricks and other weapons. Obviously, this wasn't very reassuring for the customers.

Fortunately, this kind of thing doesn't happen anymore. The government stepped in and got the violence under control. Now the taxi drivers just attack tourists' wallets. To avoid the worst of it, don't use the taxi stands at Central station or Leidseplein. Some of these driverswill simply refuse short trips, others will quote outrageously high fares, even though all taxis are metered and they are legally required to use them. Even if you convince the driver to use the meter, there is a chance he'll take a circuitous route – something that is hard to check as the city road network is very confusing – and you will have to pay €15 or more. No trip within the historic center should cost more than €10 during normal business hours. Mind you, there are night surcharges.

A good way to avoid all this when you arrive at Centraal station and want a cab is to pre-booking one. Regular taxi prices start at €2.89 and then add €2.12 per kilometer and €0.35 per minute. All taxis have a meter which will calculate the price. These work; don't believe them when they say they don't. You can also go for a fixed rate but I recommend you follow the meter, despite what the cab drivers may say.

Unlicensed and illegal cabbies operate mainly in Amsterdam Zuidoost, Leidseplein, the Prinsengracht and the Rembrandt Square. These aren't easily recognized as such, and most certainly don't drive Mercedes cars like the regular cabbies do. They are known as snorders and can be reached by mobile phone. They are cheaper, but be aware that they have a bit of a bad reputation, so unless you are experienced it might be best to avoid their services.

Another option, of course, is Uber. I personally haven't used this service, but a lot of people swear by it, saying it's a great way to travel and cheaper to boot. Still, I might think twice about getting into one when I'm alone and it's late.

By Car? In the center of Amsterdam? You must be crazy!

If you've come to Amsterdam by car, good on you, but for god's sake, don't drive it into the center of town! The city has purposefully tried to make it hard to drive around the center, and boy, have they succeeded! The plethora of dead ends, one way streets and confusing directions will frustrate you no end. The bicyclist and their utter disdain for foreigners trying to navigate the city will push your blood pressure through the roof. And the prices for parking spaces – certainly among the highest in the world – will plunder your wallet like a Somali pirate on a pleasure cruise. It's not, in other words, an adventure for the faint hearted.

A much better idea is to park your car at one of the park and rides, scattered around the city's edge and then take trams or metros into town. This will only cost you €8 a day, unlike some spots in town which will put you back almost that much per hour. They are actually quite easy to find, as you'll see big P+R signs on all the major freeways coming into town. Just follow one of those, grab your suitcases and take public transport into the city's heart.

If that doesn't float your boat and you are willing to pay, it's probably best to aim for one of the parking garages in town. If you aren't, then you can try finding a spot in Amsterdam Noord (north) where parking is still free. Of course, then you might need to take a ferry, but the first couple of dozen times there's nothing wrong with doing that (note, as mentioned, some ferries stop running between midnight and the morning, so if you want to leave in the middle of the night, this might not be the best strategy).

Chapter 6: Shopping

Most places are either really big and therefore have a large variety of shops, or are very small and therefore easy to shop in. Not many are both. Amsterdam is an exception, in that it is both small enough that it's all walkable and yet receives enough visitors that it can support the niche shops of a much bigger metropolis. This makes it a shopper's paradise, where you can buy antiques, designer clothes, books, diamonds, and anything else your heart may desire. In terms of fashion, though it isn't quite Milan or Paris, it isn't far off, with the dedicated shopper able to find everything from high fashion and hip stores to secondhand bargains.

Kalverstraat and Leidsestraat – shopping at the heart of the city center

There are several "Amsterdam shopping corridors" in the city and each one has its own specialties. What's more, many of them seem designed to link up, so you can keep walking and shopping for hours on end. If this is what you're after, you should start your shop-a-thon by heading form Centraal Station into Nieuwendijk (whose shops are a bit dingy). If you go right, you'll hit the Haarlemmerstraat, which is a great shopping street with fantastic oddball shops, but does kind of peter out after a while (and that's not what I promised you). Instead, head left, towards the Kalverstraat, for which you have to cross the Dam.

The Kalverstraat, which was named after the Kalvermarkt ("calves market") that was held here until the 17th century, is lined with shops selling competitively priced products. As is often the case in Europe, there is no car or bicycle traffic here, just shoppers – but there are many of those, so don't expect to be running any races. Also to be found here are two of the city's shopping malls (the city doesn't have that many), the Kalvertoren and the Magna Plaza and several big department stores, such as the Bonneterie, V&D and not far from the Kalverstraat, at the Dam, the Bijenkorf.

At the end of the Kalverstraat, by the Muntplein, is the flower market, where you can buy all sorts of tulips, narcissus and other kinds of flowers I don't know the names of. They also sell flower bulbs, ready to be taken home, so you can find out how green your thumbs are. One thing to note for the financially restricted, this area is aimed at tourists and not the cheapest place to buy flowers in Amsterdam! For those you need to head out of the center, for example to the Albert Cuyp market.

The flower market is not part of the shop-a-thon route, though. For that, instead of heading straight onto the flower market when you're on the Kalverstraat, you need to turn right into the Heiligeweg, or Holy Way. If you follow that to its end you'll see the Leidsestraat, which is another pedestrian shopping street, where you can find many popular brands along with souvenir shops. Again, this street is only for pedestrians, though mind the trams that run through the middle (the metal rails kind of give them away). Follow this street down to the Leidseplein, where there are many cafes, a prestigious BMW Mini showroom and an Apple Store, along with several cinemas, theaters and clubs.

P.C. Hooftstraat and the CornelisSchuytstraat – for the well-heeled shopper

From the Leidseplein it's actually quite easy to get to the P.C. Hooftstraat, which you could say is the Rodeo Drive of Amsterdam, with its modest architecture and the best (and most expensive) shops in town. All the big luxury brands are to be found here. Heck, I would even argue that if it's not here, it's not really a luxury brand, though don't quote me on that. How do you get there from the Leidseplein? Head down the Weteringschans, turn right at the big pillars that mark the entrance to the Max Euweplein (it looks like an entrance to a shopping mall, but it isn't), pass the Holland Casino and the Hard Rock, cross the water, then turn left again instead of heading into the Vondel park. You'll see it on your right hand side. You can also just ask somebody who's wearing the latest designer clothing – they're bound to know. This street does have traffic, though generally not that much.

To head onwards from here, dive into the Vondel Park at the end of this street, walk along a few hundred meters, turn left out of the park, turn right again at the Van Eeghenstraat and take your first left, you'll end up at the CornelisSchuytstraat! (Told you this was a shop-a-thon)This street rivals the P.C. Hoofstraat for price and has everything the discerning shopper might need – like the best quality food, cosmetics and wine, but also a flower shop, several design and gadgets shops and good cafés (give yourself a treat, after all, you've walked quite a distance by now!) Christie's auction house is nearby and the Amsterdam Hilton, famous for the Yoko Ono and John Lennon stay, is just two hundred meters further.Unfortunately, that's where the shop-a-thon ends. The rest of the streets are a little more scattered.

Noordermarktand TheNegenStraatjes

If you're in town on a Saturday, then you've got to head down to the Noordermarkt, to witness (and shop at) the Saturday's Farmer's Market. This is potentially the best place to pick up organic food and specialty food items in town. These aren't the only thingsyou can buy there, with many vintage goods on sale as well. Though most of the shopping in the center is very touristy, this one is mainly for the locals (less so after being mentioned in this guide, of course). Once you're done shopping it's a great idea to have a seat at one of the many terraces, have some Dutch apple pie, and watch the crowd roll by. Do be aware that this is a market and as such gets started early. In my experience, it's either go to the market on Saturday or go clubbing on Friday, you can't really do (or should I say enjoy?) both.

Last but not least is the Negenstraatjes, which I've already mentioned, but is worth mentioning again, as it's possibly the most interesting shopping area in town. The nine Small Streets are actually three streets crossing two canals – the Herengracht and Keizersgracht, and as three times three makes nine, you now know where the name comes from! Full of small fashion shops, nice restaurants, coffee bars, bookshops, interior decoration stores and hairdressers, The Nine Small Straatjes are a hip place to go indeed! What's more, there are a lot of specialty shops located here as well, including such things as a chocolate shop and a board game shop, so it's worth taking a look if you're after something specific.

Chapter 7: The Nightlife – a city of (red) lights

You can say a lot of things about Amsterdam, but that the nightlife is boring isn't one of them. There are over a thousand cafes, bars and restaurants, there are dozens of clubs, each catering to their own kind of audience and there are the coffeeshops to boot, to not even mention the kinkier exploits in the Red Light district. Really, if parties are your thing, but you can't find what you're looking for in Amsterdam, I wonder if it can be found at all.In truth, the best thing to do if you want to know where to go is go online and look it up, as every club and every bar doesn't just caters to a different kind of audience, but tends to attract different crowds on different nights.What I can provide here, however, is an idea of some of the areas you can go visit and let you pick your poison when you're there.

Leidseplein

The Leisdeplein, at the end of the Leidsestraat is probably one of the best known bar and clubbing areas in town. There are a few bars on the square itself, but I wouldn't advise most of those unless you've just successfully sold a startup to Google. Instead, head down the KorteLeidsedwarsstraat (the short Leidse cross street) or the Lange Leidsedwarsstraat (ditto, but then the long version). There are a lot of bars and restaurants here and though many are of the cheaper variety where taste is not a premium, there are some places that are slightly more upscale. One example is the Up Club, which is on the KorteLeidsedwardsstraat. On the good nights the place has two rooms open, with different DJs spinning different sets in them.

Leidseplein (By Kleon3 (Own work) CC BY-SA 4.0, via Wikimedia Commons)

You can also find the 'De Melkweg' or the Milky Waynear the Leidseplein, which is a club that's garnered quite a reputation over the years. It is just a hop, skip and a jump down the Lijnsbaangracht. On the way there you will, in fact, also pass the Sugar factory, which is another great club to go, especially on the Sunday night, when they have the Wicked Jazz

Sounds, which in my experience is just an awesome way to make sure you show up for work on Monday hungover. The club 'De Paradiso' is in the other direction, down the Weteringschans. This converted church has been housing parties since the 60s. It has life performances, club nights, a massive balcony from which you can look down into the crowd, and huge numbers of kooky parties. Some of these things are so big or so alternative that you might want to check in advance if they're for you (or if there are tickets available).

Alternatively, you can head down the Marnixstraat a few hundred meters, to find another group of bars which are well liked among the posher student population of Amsterdam. These bars are on the right hand side and if you've reached the bridge, you've gone too far.

The Red Light District

On the weekends this area pulls the party goers in like moths to red flames. The district itself is packed with bars for people to gather their Dutch courage to chat to one of the skimpily dressed ladies behind the glass. There are also a large number of hostels here, catering to the backpacking crowd that comes through town. Note that many of these hostels have rules that do not allow people over a certain age to stay there. Ageist, I know, but nonetheless true.

Bordering the Red Light on the west is the 'Warmoestraat', which has no prostitutes on it, but does have a huge number of bars, which specifically cater to the younger traveling crowd. Some of these bars are cheap, others are more expensive, so make sure you check if it's for you before you head in. There's one interesting little coffeeshop here, called Café Hill Street Blues. During warm days (as defined by the Dutch, so you might need a coat) they open up the windows downstairs, which means if the seats are free you can smoke a joint looking out over the water, which isn't three feet away.Another popular destination inside the Red Light District, on the OudezijdsAchterburgwal, is the Banana Bar for drinks, and the Banana Club, for its erotic dancing, as it's more affordable than some of the other destinations on the road. For €60 you get one hour to drink as much as you like in the Banana Bar, while for €25 you get a beer and a striptease show (more strip than tease) in the Banana Club.

Rembrandt Plein

This is another great destination for a party, though you won't find too many locals here during the early evening, mainly because the prices on the square are, once again, exceedingly high, at night the clubs are a good mix of both tourists and people from Amsterdam. Just like with the Leidseplein, it has got a lot of bars and clubs, but it's more centrally located. Some great clubs to choose from are Club Rain, Escape and studio 80, all located at or near the square. Another great choice, if you're looking for something different, is Coco's Outback. This Australian-themed bar has a cocktail hour, where expensive suddenly becomes affordable. Be careful, though, it also has a karaoke night, which is something almost always better avoided.

The main gay street, the Reguliersdwarstraat, is also to be found here, though it has to be said it has taken a bit of a hit in recent years, with many younger gay people choosing other destinations (as in other cities) to go visit. Still, there are a lot of cute little bars and restaurants that, though they cater to the gay crowd, are generally just as welcoming to the straight community.

Chapter 8: The Museums, big and small, mainstream and odd

Amsterdam prides itself on being a cultural city and as such has numerous museums, both big and small, main stream, like the Rembrandt museum, the Rijksmuseum and the Stedelijk museum, and kooky, like the handbag museum and the sex museum. With more than fifty museums scattered around the city, there's likely to be something for everybody – even the stoners have been provided for, with their very own Hash, Marijuana and Hemp museum! Now if they only were sober enough to find the place.   .

Be aware that the more popular destinations, like the Anne Frank House and the Stedelijk museum, can get very crowded in the summer peak season, so it's worth buying tickets in advance or getting there offpeak (i.e. very early in the morning, or – as many are open until 10 o'clock at night – in the evenings). Otherwise, with destinations like the Anne Frank House, you'll find yourself in line longer than you are in the museum!

That can't be the idea, can it? Also, if you're planning to visit a few, a Museumkaart is a very good idea. This card represents a personal pass to enter more than 400 museums in the Netherlands. It is valid one year and it costs €59.90 for adults and €32.45 for those under 18. The price includes a one-time starting fee of €4.95, which has to be paid only the first time you purchase such a card (just in case you decide to come back). This might sound expensive, but as many museums will put you back €15, if you're there for only four days and visit two museums a day, you'll end up ahead.

Alternatively, you can get an I AMsterdam City Card, which allows you to get into some museums and GVB public transport for free for as long as the ticket lasts. Check the terms and conditions! The Stedelijk museum, for example, is not free. Instead you only get a €2.50 discount. These cards are valid for 24, 48 or 72 hours. For more information on the I AMsterdam City Card visit their website.

Museum Plein – Stedelijk museum, Rijks Museum and the Van Gogh museum

So, where do you go for the Museums? Well, Museumplein (Museum Square) is a pretty good place to start! This square is located at the southwestern side of the Rijksmuseum, near the Leidseplein. The northeastern part of the square is bordered by the very large and very impressive Rijksmuseum, which only recently came out of a ten-year renovation, which is quite funny as this means that the renovation actually took longer than the original construction (nine years). How does that work? The building was designed by renowned Dutch architect P.J.H. Cuypers and it opened its doors in 1885. It is the largest museum in the Netherlands and gets over a one million visitors each year. That is more people than the entire population of Amsterdam. Line that many people up in a straight line and it would stretch all the way to Frankfurt!

Inside there are nearly one million objects, which – if you'd want to look at each one for about ten seconds –

would take, provided you didn't stop for bathroom breaks, more than a hundred days to view. The Rijksmuseum holds the country's largest collection of art and artifacts, including 40 Rembrandts and four Vermeers. The collection was started when William V began to acquire pieces just for the hell of it (he probably didn't think so), and has been growing ever since. It includes Dutch paintings from the 15th century until the nineteen hundreds, as well as decorative and Asian art, which has its own newly-build pavilion.

But the biggest draw is the collection of Golden Age paintings, such as Rembrandt's Night Watch, as well as Vermeer's Kitchen Maid and Woman Reading a Letter, you can also find works by such artists as Jacob de Wit, Frans Hals and Ferdinand Bol. Make sure you check out the fantastic silver and porcelain, 17th- and early 18th-century dolls' houses, which have been furnished and decorated to give you a glimpse into how people used to live back then. There are eighteenth- and nineteenth - century paintings, statues and lacquer work. Then there are ceramics, jewelry, art objects from Asia, and weapons. Exhausted yet? Head over to the beautiful garden, filled with Golden Age gateways and architectural fragments. It is an oasis of tranquility, where you can give both your feet and your mind a rest.

And who could visit Amsterdam without looking at the Van Gogh Museum? Nobody, apparently, considering how often people stop me on the street to ask me where the damned thing is! Though he only lived in Amsterdam for a short time, the city somehow felt this should be the place to build his museum. Perhaps that's because the man couldn't stop moving around. I looked up how many places he'd lived and stopped counting after about 20 addresses. That's quite something; especially considering moving around was a lot harder back then. For one thing, they didn't have mover trucks, or motorized vehicles of any kind, really. Did he just carry his paintings under his arm?

Photo Credit 28 "Van Gogh Museum" by Warrox Licensed under CC BY 2.5 via Wikimedia Commons

The museum is housed in one of the few modern buildings in this area of Amsterdam and houses the largest collection of works by Vincent van Gogh – more than 200 paintings, 500 drawings and 700 of his letters. Some of Van Gogh's most famous paintings, like the Aardappeleters (The Potato Eaters) and Zonnebloemen (Sunflowers) are present here as well.

Not seen enough yet? Well, then head over to Stedelijk Museum, located right next door. This museum, which is Amsterdam's most important museum of modern art, opened its doors in 1895 and is as old as museum square itself. The permanent collection consists of works from artists like Piet Mondriaan, Karel Appel, and Kazimir Malevich. For most of the 20th century, Stedelijk directors somehow managed to snap up work from hot new art movements before the rest of the world was really taking notice, such as paintings and other work by CoBrA and De Stijl. There's a rich collection of design and applied art, too, with video art and other new works getting showcased prominently. A new composite extension was opened in 2012. People call it the bathtub and its strange shape is a perfect example of why some people love modern art and other people think it's a load of horse manure.

Anne Frank House, FOAM and the Ajax Museum

A visit to Amsterdam wouldn't be complete without visiting Anne Frank House in the heart of the city. This museum was the actual hiding place where Anne Frank wrote her famous diary during the World War II. It is on display, as a part of the Anne Frank House's permanent exhibition. If you are planning to visit the museum, I heartily advise you to actually read her diary (don't worry, they've made copies), as otherwise the effect is kind of lost. After all, the museum's main attraction is only a few rooms hidden behind a swinging book case. With the book fresh in your mind, however, it becomes so much more – you can sense the fear and the frustration, as two families spent two years cooped up here, hoping the Nazis wouldn't find them. (Spoiler alert: they didn't make it). As noted before, choose your time of arrival wisely! If you don't, you will spend more time waiting in front of the building then you spend inside.

The FOAM Photography Museum is another great location. Not only is it an internationally renowned museum that exhibits all genres of photography, it also acts as a creative hub where photographers can meet and participate in forums and symposiums. It really is well worth checking out, as it showcases some of photography's biggest names, including Diane

Arbus, Helen Levitt, Anton Corbijn, Alex Prager and CyTwombly. Alongside these large-scale artists, the brightly lit rooms of this revamped canal-house are filled with work from upcoming talents. Want to know more about what's actually being displayed in the museum? Make sure you're there on Thursdays at 18:30, as then the museum offers a free tour.

For fans of Dutch football (or 'soccer' for the less sophisticated among you), the Ajax museum is an absolute must – though if you're a fan, you no doubt already knew that. This wonderful museum covers the rich history of one of the most renowned clubs in the Netherlands, as well as displaying many photographs, memorabilia, trophies and videos documenting their greatest players and triumphs. Football is an incredibly important sport to the Dutch, whose national team is reputedly the best team to never have won the world cup (a bitter-sweet label indeed). And Ajax has, over the decades, been one of the most important contributors to that team.

Photo Credit 31:"Ajax's international trophies displayed in the club's museum" by Jason Licensed under GFDL via Wikimedia Commons

Offbeat museums – the Sex Museum, the Hash, Marijuana and Hemp Museum, and the handbag museum

But why would you only go visit the mainstream museums? This city, after all, has a history off leftist thinkers, oddball ideas and 'creative' policies, many of which can be explored through the city's stranger museums. One that immediately catches most people's attention is the Sex Museum, or "The temple

169

of Venus". The Sex Museum throughout more than 20 years of its existence, has not only collected many hundreds of interesting pieces of art, unique objects and rare old photographs, but has managed to avoid becoming just another pornographic sideshow. And this is something to be applauded. After all, we've already got the Red Light District for that kind of stuff. Why would we need a museum to be dedicated to it as well?

Another great and unusual museum is the Hash, Marihuana & Hemp Museum. These are in fact two small museums, which you can visit for the price of one. Both are located at OudezijdsAchterburgwal, one of the canals of the Red Light District. The first one, called 'The Museum', covers different uses of the hemp plant and some of its varieties used for recreational purposes. The second one is called the Hemp Gallery and puts an accent on civilized use of cannabis, its history and tradition in arts and argues that for the wider use of hemp as a fabric. A small art gallery where individual shows of painters and photographers are housed, is located at the back of the exhibit.

And then there's the museum of bags and purses, located at the Herengracht 573 which, you will no doubt be surprised to discover, is dedicated to purses, handbags and their history. Now I'm not suggesting that this will blow your mind, on the other hand, the cues are small and for a little of your time and a little pocket money (€12.50 for an adult) you have some great facts and stories to tell at future cocktail parties. I mean, what's the chance that there will be somebody else there who knows interesting and odd facts about hand bags from the 16th century? Not high, right? One way to know more than anybody else about a subject is to spend years studying it. Another way is to simply make sure that the topic is esoteric enough that nobody else knows anything else about it! They also do high tea.

Chapter 9: When to Visit – festivals in the city of Amsterdam

There are a lot of great festivals in the Netherlands. Here are a few, scattered across the year, to check out. Do take a look, as not preparing for some of these (or not knowing they are going on) can ruin your vacation.

Kings day – or one of the best festivals in the world

Recently renamed King's day, after the queen mother abdicated her throne, this day, on the 27th of April, is a fantastic day to be in the city if you love a party (and a horrible day to be there if you don't). For a night and a day the whole town goes absolutely insane (all of the Netherlands does, in fact). Everybody dresses up in costumes and the Netherland's national color, a horrendous orange that seems designed to offend the eyes, then goes out onto the street to drink, dance and have a good time. Early on during the day people sell furniture, knickknacks and random things in a giant flea market that is a bargain hunter's paradise. Mind you, it's important to be there early if you want to pick up anything interesting, as the good stuff gets snapped up quickly by antique dealers, connoisseurs and the dedicated. Later on, you'll often find there's only junk, and children playing instruments (generally cutely but poorly), left over.

By Tom Morris (Own work) CC BY 3.0 via Wikimedia Commons

Later on in the day, people start drinking, quite heavily it has to be said, taking drugs (it's true) and going crazy, but in a very Dutch way – there are rarely any fights and the mood is jovial, friendly and inclusive. On specially nominated squares clubs organize open parties, where world famous DJs spin, bands play and people go out of their heads. This goes on all day and well into the night and is a fantastic opportunity to see what the Dutch people get up to when they really get it in their heads to party.

Some things to note! As the city floods with tourists from other cities in Amsterdam and other countries (the city population supposedly doubles during these days) it is very hard indeed to get a hotel during this time, so if you want to come, make sure you book far ahead. Also, as the city is so crowded, the main throughways are absolutely jam packed and you'll only be able to walk through them at a snail's pace. This means distances that would normally take you only ten minutes can now easily take more than half an hour or more. The trick is to use the back streets, which are also crowded, but still walkable. So take a map and study it carefully if you want to go any distance whatsoever. Otherwise I promise you, you will get fed up. I once saw a lady get so frustrated she started using her baby carriage as a battering ram. The baby was still in it.

Finally, during daylight hours you'll see many children on the street and your own children might enjoy the festival as well (it is a crazy but jovial affair). Later on, however, after the people have been drinking for a while, it might be better to retreat to your hotel and turn on a Disney movie, as these hours are more suitable for an adult crowd, with the little people possibly finding it a little overwhelming.

Gay Pride – all dressed up in very little

Another great festival to attend for those of a more liberal bend is gay pride, which happens in early August (August 4th in 2016). Note that you don't actually need to be gay to enjoy this festival; it is very enjoyable for straight people as well, (though you do have to be able to accept men dressed in very skimpy outfits making out with each other). During this day the Prinsengracht gets occupied by hundreds of floats and boats, sponsored by everybody from the police to political parties, on which the gay community demonstrates their pride at being who they are. Some of these floats are absolutely fantastic and the fact that the gay community gets – even if only for one day – to not hide their sexuality, but instead display it openly is wonderful (in recent years there have been some anti-gay sentiments in the city, which is unfortunate as it used to be a safe haven for this minority group). Then, when the parade is done, everybody retreats to the squares around the canals and parties into the night.

In many ways, Gay Pride is much like King's day with the same kind of great atmosphere and positive attitudes, only generally with better weather, as August is warmer in the Netherlands, and smaller, in that it doesn't take over the entire city. Many locals actually prefer this festival, as it doesn't get quite as crazy, doesn't bring in quite as many tourists, and doesn't deposit quite as much trash on the street. The city, in other words, still partially functions around this festival, while on King's Day everything grinds to an absolute halt.

Which should you choose? I have absolutely no idea. They both have their merits. I think ultimately what matters is when you have time and whether you find immense crowds or men kissing harder to deal with. For both, renting a boat and going out on the water can be a great deal of fun.

Grachtenfestival – or classical music on the canals

This is another great festival, for those who prefer not to drink till they drop. For a few days in the middle of August (in 2016 it will run from the 12th till the 21st), across the city there is classical music performed live and out in the open. Obviously, the vibe is completely different from either Kings Day or Gay Pride, but it is still an absolutely fantastic event to visit, with classical musicians coming in from all over the world to take part. Different days have different artists performing at different venues. Often there are paid seats available, but you can just as easily stand, or sit along the canal banks and enjoy the music for free. Note that with some of the more popular performances, the canal sides can pack out completely, so come early if you want to see something. Want to learn more? Just type 'Grachtenfestival' into a search engine! The main site is also available in English.

Museum Night – party among the paintings!

One night in November Amsterdam has this fantastic event called 'Museum nacht'. For one night, the museums open their doors till deep into the night (2 AM), even while all the bars and restaurants hold cultural events. There are even some parties in the museums themselves! For €18.50 you've got a ticket to more than 50 museums, as well as a discount on public transportation. What's more, this is still a very Dutch event. So Dutch, in fact, that the website for it doesn't even have an English version. The idea is to expose a younger audience to the cultural events going on in the Netherlands, but of course it's also a wonderful opportunity for tourists to enjoy a lot of museums on the cheap.

New Years – bring a coat

A lot of people like New Years in the Netherlands. It's not my personal favorite, but I can understand where they're coming from. The Dutch certainly shoot off a lot of fireworks. Make sure you ask around where the best displays are. There's one guy (group?) who always shoots off a great display in front of the Anne Frank House, then there's another display over the water of the IJ. If you can avoid it, don't cross the Dam. This place is a bit of a war zone after midnight, with people throwing firework at each other and whoever crosses the square.

The least enjoyable thing about New Years is that every single bar, club and party location suddenly has a cover charge. And it is steep! €50 euros, for a bar that normally has free entry is quite common. Of course, there are exceptions, but as a tourist it is hard to know where those are. If you can make it to the city a few days early and have the gift of the gab, you might be able to get yourself invited to a crazy house party. Then you're really cooking with gas. New Year really is a lot of fun with a group of Dutch people counting down the seconds. Getting stuck outside, in the cold (it's December), with nowhere to go, on the other hand, isn't quite as much fun. In other words, to have a great new year in Amsterdam, some preparation is required.

Chapter 10: Conclusion

Amsterdam, with its ancient streets, canals and hidden corners, is among the most beautiful and quirky cities in the world. And if you were looking for more reasons for a visit, hopefully this guide has provided them, for there is so much more to the city than just being able to spark up a joint. There is culture, there is history, and there are the thousands of examples of former (and perhaps even current) greatness.

This guide has only covered some of the city's stories in depth, while hinting at a whole host more, but there is so much to explore. And, in truth, the city deserves your time, with every hour invested in exploring its hidden corners offering up secrets that you could never have guessed at. The truth is, in Amsterdam more history has been forgotten than most other cities have ever had.

And then there are the people, of course, with their straightforwardness, their honesty and (as you might have noticed form this guide) their irreverent humor. I hope it has entertained you more than it has offended and I hope it has made it so that you feel an urge to meet more of these tall non-germans in person. Enjoy your time in Amsterdam and if you discover something new, let me know. I'm always looking to learn more about this wonderful city.

PS: Can I Ask You For A Special Favor?

Hopefully this guidebook has given you some ideas about what to do during your stay in Amsterdam!!

We would like to ask you for a favor, would you be kind enough to leave a review for this book on Amazon? It'd be greatly appreciated!

Thanks a lot.

Preview of "Switzerland - By Locals"

We edit and publish travel guides from several cities in the world, all written by locals. When you plan your next destiny, please check on Amazon if we are covering that city already. If not, we will probably writing about it soon, please give us some time.

We would like to give you an advance of our Switzerland Guide, which is very special. Please take a look:

Chapter 1: My Switzerland - Where scenic wonders prevail

Switzerland is a country of incredible contrasts, from the dense pine forests and vast mountains, to the rolling hills and glossy rivers. Switzerland or the Swiss Confederation has much to offer to those in search of culture, modern amenities and historical treasures. Switzerland is situated in Western and Central Europe, and consists of 26 cantons. Each canton has a high level of independence. The country also has one of the world's most powerful economies.

Bordered by Italy to the south, Germany to the north, France to the west, and Austria and Liechtenstein to the east, Switzerland is one of the most interesting European countries and boasts its own character, history and unique beautiful cities. For most, the gateway to Switzerland is Bern. The city is renowned for its traditional folk entertainment and vibrant nightlife.

With so much to do, see, and experience, it is really hard to narrow down the long list of reasons to visit my country. Beyond its marvelous capital, Switzerland has other major cities worth visiting, including Zürich and Geneva. Both Zürich and Geneva are ranked among the world's top ten cities for the highest quality of life. Interestingly, Switzerland is not a member state of the European Union. A relatively small country of just eight million inhabitants, Switzerland appeals to a wide range of visitors: from backpackers and outdoor enthusiasts to history buffs. In addition, Switzerland is a mesmerizing destination for winter sports enthusiasts. Skiing, snowboarding, ice hockey and mountaineering are the most popular sports in the country. Being a landlocked country, it is divided between the Alps, the Swiss Plateau or Central Plateau and the Jura mountains. Switzerland boasts some incredible natural landscapes, and has more than 1500 lakes. Although Bern, Zürich and Geneva remain the star attractions in Switzerland, beyond them lays a diverse and absolutely beautiful country worth exploring. A land of mountains, lakes glaciers, and four languages, – Switzerland truly has it all. No wonder it's one of the world's most prestigious destinations.

Chapter 2: Climate & When to go

A popular year-round destination, Switzerland has a fairly moderate climate with warm summers and cold winters. The changeable weather varies greatly throughout the country. Northeastern corners of Switzerland generally have warm summers and cold winters with rainfall evenly distributed throughout the year and snowfall likely in winter.

However, the weather can change rapidly, especially in the Alpine regions. Some regions in the east usually have much colder winters and hotter summers, while the southeastern parts of the country have longer and warmer summers. In the higher Alpine areas temperatures tend to be low. Generally, the hottest months are July and August, though these are also the most popular months in terms of tourist numbers, so it is recommended to book your accommodations several months in advance. Summer is generally the peak season, when it is warm and sunny across much of the country. Summer is also the most popular and most expensive time to visit. Summers in Switzerland are usually warm and quite pleasant, especially in the southernmost canton of Ticino. Hotels and sights are usually overflowing with tourists. However, you can escape the crowds if you visit during the autumn months. Autumn is really a great time to visit Switzerland. During this time of year, prices will generally be lower than they are during the peak season. September and October are the ideal months for a tour of Switzerland.

Winter in Switzerland is also a very popular time to visit, with travelers flocking from all over the world to take advantage of the country's fantastic ski resorts and outdoor attractions. If you are visiting at this time, expect inflated prices. In contrary, it is cheaper to visit some smaller towns and villages in winter. Keep in mind that some of the most popular ski resorts get crowded during the winter, so make sure to book your accommodations at least a month in advance to ensure a fair price. If you don't mind the cold, winter can be the best time to visit Switzerland.

Spring is another great time to visit my country. It is a great season to start planning your vacation. Spring is usually chilly, so you can expect slightly cool yet comfortable temperatures. If you are planning to visit the mountains, it's best to take waterproof gear and extra layers with you, no matter what the time of year. To be completely honest. there is never a bad time to visit Switzerland. To sum it up, the best times to visit Switzerland are from April to June and from September to December. The conclusion is quite obvious; Switzerland is absolutely fantastic year round.

inattention or otherwise, by any usage or abuse of any policies, processes, or directions contained within is the solitary and utter responsibility of the recipient reader. Under no circumstances will any legal responsibility or blame be held against the publisher for any reparation, damages, or monetary loss due to the information herein, either directly or indirectly.

Respective authors own all copyrights not held by the publisher.

The information herein is offered for informational purposes solely, and is universal as so. The presentation of the information is without contract or any type of guarantee assurance.

The trademarks that are used are without any consent, and the publication of the trademark is without permission or backing by the trademark owner. All trademarks and brands within this book are for clarifying purposes only and are the owned by the owners themselves, not affiliated with this document.

Made in the USA
San Bernardino, CA
14 February 2019